Home Wasn't Built in a Day

*Growing up in County Limerick –
Recollections of a Rural Irish Childhood*

PADDY CRONIN

Copyright ©2007 Paddy Cronin

The moral right of Paddy Cronin to be identified
as the author of this work has been asserted.

First published in the Republic of Ireland 2007

All rights reserved.
No part of this publication may be reproduced or transmitted
in any form or by any means, digital, electronic or mechanical,
including photography, filming, video recording, photocopying,
or by any information storage or retrieval system,
without prior written permission.

The paper used in the manufacture of this book is made
from wood pulp from managed forests. For every tree felled,
at least one is planted, thereby renewing natural resources.

ISBN 978-0-9556656-0-8

Printed and bound in the UK by
J.H. Haynes & Co Ltd, Sparkford, Somerset

Paddy Cronin was born and bred in Askeaton, County Limerick.
He lives in Ballyvocogue, Cappagh, Askeaton, with his wife Jackie.

Paddy is the author of several books on local history and is a regular contributor to newspapers, magazines and local radio.

*

Other publications by Paddy Cronin
The Auld Town 1995
Aubrey de Vere - The Bard of Curragh Chase 1997
Michael D. Ryan - The People's Poet 1998
Eas Céad Tine- The Waterfall of the Hundred Fires 1999
St. Mary's Catholic Church - A Celebration of Faith 2001

*

AUTHOR'S NOTE

This book is a combination of memories and stories that were handed down to me by my late parents, family and friends. Stories that have been told to me, I have retold them as accurately as my memory would allow. A few names have been changed to protect anonymity.

ACKNOWLEDGEMENTS

Family and friends have been my main inspiration in writing this book. They kept encouraging me to continue on, assuring me that there was light at the end of the tunnel. The legacy of the many stories told to me by my late parents has greatly encouraged me. I always felt that such wonderful tales had to be retold and written down for posterity, lest they be forgotten.

My friend Seamus Ryan, now living in Alameda, California, motivated me from the very beginning. Many hours and late nights were spent on the phone to USA, with Seamus filling me in with some forgotten details of one of his many yarns.

My aunt, Katie Sheahan, who was always my first port of call for reminiscing, clarification and delving into the archives, gave me immeasurable assistance.

A special word of thanks to Mike Kenneally, Creeves, Askeaton; Michael D. Ryan, Bawnreagh, Askeaton; Micheal Downey, Pallaskenry; Biddy Staff, Pallaskenry; Norah Staff, Pallaskenry; Mary Ellen Speran, Dooradoyle, Limerick. Their recollections and willingness to share information was greatly appreciated.

I was extremely grateful for the assistance of the Limerick City Library, and to the Library at Mary Immaculate College for allowing me to use their archives.

A special word of thanks also to Myra Hayes, Fr. Russell Rd, Dooradoyle, Limerick, Mrs. Una Nolan, Alhambra, California, USA, Brian Mangan, Askeaton and Frank O'Callaghan, Askeaton

Paddy Cronin

for reading my drafts and encouraging me to continue with the project. Thanks also to Hugh Stancliffe, Ashford Lodge, Ballagh, Co. Limerick, the Irish representative of J H Haynes, for organising the book layout and printing.

I would also like to thank best selling novelist, Grace Wynne-Jones for writing the Foreword and for her encouragement and kind words.

To my wife Jackie for being there always, with me and for me. Her constructive criticism was always valued and taken on board. Also, to my son Patrick for his understanding and patience.

When I needed a Graphic Designer to create the cover of the book, I was delighted to call upon my daughter Helena. Her creation was finalised just days before her son TJ, our first grandson, was born. Thanks also to her husband Tomás for being so understanding while there were far more pressing matters on his mind.

Finally, I would like to say a very sincere thank you to my sponsor, Cois Sionna Credit Union, Askeaton. Without your very generous financial assistance I would have been unable to publish this book. Congratulations to you on forty very successful years of serving the local community of Askeaton and the wider hinterland of West Limerick.

Paddy Cronin

FOREWORD

Paddy Cronin is a special man and this is a special book. He has already established his reputation as an eloquent and successful author. And now he has chosen to share his own story with us and it is a heartfelt one, which is truthful, brave and entrancing.

This is a fascinating and entertaining tale but it is more than that. It is an exploration of shelter and starkness, belonging and growing. The Ireland Paddy evokes in these pages is very different from the Ireland of today. These are no rose-tinted recollections. Emigration and bereavement influenced Paddy's early years. Thankfully they did not dent his spirit. He didn't have an easy childhood but he had a good one because he was loved and loved well.

There is much to make one smile and marvel in these pages. A sheer sense of fun and youthful exploration. In rural communities people often made and were their own entertainment. Larger than life individuals abounded and so did the tales about their exploits. Young Paddy eventually discovered why Michaelin Sheahan sewed conkers into his pants. And as for, Tom Donovan, well he had his own views on interior decoration and wallpapered his house with pages from The Irish Press. Entertaining nicknames were commonplace and a number of men, such as 'Mick the Robin' found themselves named after different breeds of birds.

Paddy Cronin

One is impressed by how much Paddy noticed and how much he now remembers. Many of the characters honoured in this tale are more colourful and frequently more humorous than anything available on TV in multi-channel Celtic Tiger Ireland. It seems that even as a small boy he was a keen and skilled observer who cherished the lustre of detail.

He was also sensitive young lad who had to make peace with his frequent bewilderment. Superstition was rife and priests patrolled the hedgerows for courting couples. There were strange rules and strictures and at school Paddy was told that if he went near a Protestant church during a service he would have to receive special absolution from the Bishop. The grand mysteries of life itself often shone and sometimes leaned on the small community.

At one stage his father had to emigrate to find work and when he returned on visits home he hugged his son and wept with joy at the reunion. Money was often short but his resourceful parents nourished their own sense of possibility. Job opportunities were scarce but they found them. They made a good home for Paddy and his two sisters, and their redemptive love is at the centre of this memoir.

Paddy's beloved father died when he was a boy and the pain of that loss is eloquently described. But though the family often struggled to cope with their circumstances life was about more than just survival. And faith provided a sustaining glimpse of light in the darker days.

Many of the people Paddy celebrates in these pages have passed away. One of them is his courageous and devoted mother who eventually ran her own successful shop where people also gathered to chat and even to match-make. As Paddy grew older Ireland changed and, at last, there were more opportunities. Television arrived in the town and people gathered to watch men walking on the moon.

There are many forms of love and one of them is remembering. And what we remember shows how we inhabited a time and a place. How closely we were attuned to its rhythm's, shapes, and textures. I myself was brought up in County Limerick in a rambling rectory and have very different recollections of childhood. But I too had that deep sense of place. And I can recall an Ireland that was simpler, and in other ways more complex.

Paddy remembers well, and as I have discovered myself, is a man who retains his special gift for friendship. He and my brother Vere were good friends and I know Vere would have loved to write the Foreword for this book, but sadly he passed away in July 2006 and is greatly missed. Paddy knew Vere through his mother's family connections with the de Veres of Curragh Chase. My mother Joan de Vere was brought up in that great house and my parents spent their honeymoon there. It was and is a cherished place and Paddy has celebrated the life of Aubrey de Vere in an excellent biography. Paddy's mothers people, the Sheahans, were the de Vere's chauffeurs for many years and they came to have an intimate knowledge of their comings and goings, their lives and their affections. And now I know Paddy too and feel honoured to have written this Foreword.

Vere had a well honed appreciation of a good story well told and told plenty of them himself. I know he would have also greatly admired the way Paddy writes so evocatively about the vast variety of people he met on his travels through boyhood.

And how he skilfully shares the laughter, mystery, challenges and joys of a precious place called home.

Grace Wynne-Jones

Paddy Cronin

*This book is dedicated
to the memory of my late parents*

'They had courage equal to desire'

Home Wasn't Built in a Day

'Tis the song, the sigh of the weary,
Hard times, hard times,
Come again no more
Many days you have lingered
Around my cabin door;
Oh hard times come again no more

Hard Times Come Again No More
Stephen Foster 1854

INTRODUCTION

Growing up in the 1950s and 60s rural Ireland was sometimes tough, but whatever depths we sank to, there was always someone or something that managed to salvage our sanity. Life was uncompromising with very little support outside the family unit. With the enforced absence of my father through the curse of emigration and his untimely death, my mother, a strong and deeply religious woman was forever steadfast, always there to ensure we survived. If we got through today, tomorrow would always be better and in the face of adversity, somehow my mother always won out. She was a pious woman, but so were a lot of people back then; God was all we had and the Catholic Church played a big part in our daily lives.

We were lucky that most people had a sense of humour, without which we would have been doomed. There were many characters, who with their innate sense of humour made life and day to day living exciting to say the least. There were storytellers and story makers, with tales of pishogs and superstition making sure that times were never dull. Television in the '60s awakened a new desire in us. We all wanted to be like those people in the box in the corner and the determination to better ourselves drove us on. The dancehalls or 'Ballrooms of Romance' as they were then known, were our social outlets, and finding a suitable wife was always top of the agenda.

With the influx of multinational industries in the '70s, prosperity was finally on the horizon. Rural Ireland had become a better place to live and the bad old days of the '50s and '60s had finally been extinguished. A new era of Irish life had begun.

Paddy Cronin

ONE

His parting was poignant but very much inevitable. It was February, 1958, when my father first took the emigration boat to England. Without any hope of employment at home, it very often was the only option open to the breadwinner. Home was where the heart was for most fathers, but the reality was somewhat different, as working in England was increasingly becoming the norm.

Like most Irish families of our time in the '50s and '60s, we were not blessed with the luxuries of life. Unemployment was rife, money was scarce and very few people had any extras. My mother and father always tried to do their living best for me and my two younger sisters, Mary and Breda. They always had a certain amount of grandeur about them. It was as if they wanted us to aspire to the higher things in life, aspirations that they through no fault of their own could never have reached. One thing that our parents instilled in us was a sense of integrity. 'Honesty is the best policy' was always their motto.

My mother Bridgie always said, 'Never let yourself down, always mix above yourself, and if you don't have it, or you're in poverty, do without it. Having plenty is wonderful but being happy with little is even more important.'

Home Wasn't Built in a Day

She was a woman of great sayings and proverbs. To remind us to be frugal with our food and money she would constantly say, 'Wilful waste makes woeful want.'

As children, we would often plague her to buy us something that she could not afford. We always got the same response.

'Name of God, I haven't d'itch (the itch), nor the ointment to cure it.'

This was an era when values were of a spiritual nature and self esteem was very important. Material values were almost unknown and people were more than content to earn a decent living in order to put enough food on the table for their family. Also, it was most important to live a life that was very much in keeping with the Grace of God and the teachings of the Catholic Church. A constant reminder of our Faith was the picture of Pope Pius XII which adorned the mantlepiece of almost every house. It was also the custom to bless oneself with Holy Water when leaving home; appropriately, every house had a font laden with Holy Water at the front door.

My mother also taught us that there was no such thing as a good loser. And by God, was she a woman never to 'throw in the towel.' She would tackle every problem head on and fight to the bitter end. Defeat or negativity was not in her vocabulary. As a young child growing up herself, she was well-noted in the community as a very hard and dedicated worker. Her mother died quite young, so she assumed a very senior role at home. Her family were fairly well off. They had a car hackney business which was exclusive and very profitable at the time. They were also chauffeurs to the aristocratic family, the de Veres of Curragh Chase. My mother also reared up to twenty pigs at a time. She would buy them in as little piglets, or bonamhs as they were known, and rear them 'til they were ready for O'Mara's bacon factory in Limerick city.

Our town was built on the banks of the river Deel, which is a tributary of the Shannon. For hundreds of years, fishing was one of the main sources of income and a valuable means for food. As poverty became more widespread, illegal snatching of fish from the river was rife. People had no choice. Taking the odd salmon here and there from the river, meant an extra few bob. The fishery board had many bailiffs patrolling the river, resulting in frequent prosecutions and court cases. In turn, many a father was unable to pay the fine imposed by the courts and he ended up in jail. My mother often told me that lots of poor old souls were glad to spend time inside, as they had a bed with some regular food.

The river Shannon itself, provided a good livelihood for many local fishermen, until the early 1900s. My mother told me of fishermen bringing in large catches of herring and then selling them on the local quays. All this changed on an ill-fated night in October 1917, when three local fishermen were drowned while out netting a large haul of herring. Since that tragic night, a herring was neither seen nor caught on the Shannon again. It was as if some sort of curse had befallen the area after the dreadful accident.

Times were tough and sometimes uncompromising. Mrs Collins sent her husband down to the butcher for half a pigs head and when he did not return after a few hours she began to worry. She sent her son, Dan Terry, downtown in search of him. He found his father lying on the footpath.

Home Wasn't Built in a Day

He had collapsed as a result of having a few drinks too many. Dan Terry immediately grabbed the half a head and ran home with it to his mother. He ignored his father and left him lying on the ground. When asked afterwards why did he leave his father he said, 'Nobody was going to run away with my father, but I wouldn't trust anyone with the half a head!'

My earliest recollections of home are very happy ones. As a young boy I would sit on my father's knee, he gently bouncing me up and down, singing:

Hub hub hubby horse, hub hub again,
How many miles to Dublin, three score and ten,
Will I be there in candle light, yes and back again,
Hub hub hubby horse, hub hub again.

I was born in The Alexandra Nursing Home in Limerick which was considered very elitist at the time. God only knows how my parents afforded this luxury. It was the early 1950s in Ireland, and I guess that, as the saying goes, 'the worst was yet to come.'

After I was born I was brought home to a humble little house in Mussel Lane, Askeaton. After a few months, we moved to the house I was reared in at Main Street. My mother would constantly remind me that great people came out of Mussel Lane including the ancestors of Sean Keating, the great painter, and his son Justin, who became a Government Minister.

When they brought me home from the nursing home there was great excitement in the lane. My mother told me of the many people who called to the little house to welcome the new arrival. As the excitement intensified, my father's cousin Johnny Cronin broke into verse with the Wild Colonial Boy.

> *There was a wild colonial boy, Jack Duggan was his name*
> *He was born and bred in Ireland in a place called Castlemaine*
> *He was his father's only son, his mother's pride and joy*
> *And dearly did his parents love the Wild Colonial Boy*

That song was very popular at the time as it was sung in the film, *The Quiet Man,* which was shown in cinemas all over Ireland in the year I was born. My mother liked the song as it was about a young Irish boy who left his native shore and went to Australia, where he became an outlaw, but was a champion of the poor. If the singing of that song was putting down a marker for me in the future, well then, I had some turbulent years ahead of me. Thankfully, it was only sung for its popularity at the time.

A dark cloud hung over the community for many years due to the callous and seemingly cold blooded murder of the local Parish Priest. This happened a few years before I was born; nevertheless, it was a poignant incident that nobody wanted to discuss, but at the same time was never far from people's minds. Religion was sacred and the Catholic Priest was revered and always held in the highest esteem. For many years people in the community were trying to come to terms with this terrible act, but could never find a reason or an answer.

My mother often recalled the events that occurred on that ill fated night. At nine o'clock on Sunday, January 6th 1946, the feast of Little Christmas, Father Patrick Casey was shot and died outside the front door of the Parochial

Home Wasn't Built in a Day

House. Father Casey went outside the house to investigate the barking of his dog in the grounds and was shot at from the nearby shrubbery.

Lying in a pool of blood, he called for his housekeeper, Hannah Curtin and she immediately raised the alarm. The Curate, Father Rea, who lived next door, administered the Lasts Rights and Doctor Fitzgibbon arrived only to pronounce Father Casey dead. A murder investigation immediately got under way. Hours later, a young man from nearby Borrigone called to the local Garda barracks and handed in a gun, declaring that he had shot the Priest. The following morning, John Cullinan was charged with the murder of sixty-nine year old Father Casey. The whole community was cast deep into depression and shock. All business premises and shops kept the shutters up for a number of days and every dwelling house had the blinds drawn.

So, why such a shocking tragedy? Twenty-nine year old John Cullinan had been calling to Father Casey on a regular basis, mainly to discuss the merits of Communism and the plight of the small farmer. Some years prior to this, a local branch of Saor Éire, meaning 'Free Ireland' was founded. The roots and aims of this republican organisation were based on left-wing and communist politics. Its aims were the pursuit of socialist goals on behalf of workers and working farmers. It was rumoured at the time that John Cullinan, who was a well-read man, and was a supporter of Saor Éire, was annoyed by the Catholic Church denouncing them. The Catholic Bishops of Ireland had deemed Saor Éire to be communists and as such, considered them sinful and irreligious.

It was clear that John Cullinan was not of sound mind, and at the time he was said to be suffering from delusions. John felt that he was at total loggerheads with the Priest and that his ideas and opinions were not being taken seriously, so he decided to murder him. Although charged with the murder of Father Casey, he was never actually convicted of the crime. At a special sitting of Adare court, two doctors certified him to be insane and the charge preferred against him was abandoned. John Cullinan spent the rest of his life in St. Joseph's mental hospital in Limerick city.

My parents were never great people for dates and days to remember. They could never tell me the exact date I was born. My father would say February 6th and my mother February 7th. As far as they were concerned, the actual date was of no consequence. It was the person that mattered. It wasn't until I came to get married, and required a copy of my birth certificate, that I was able to pinpoint the date of my birth. It was, in fact, February 5th. Ironically, neither my mother nor my father were right.

When I was just three years old, my father brought me to the top of a hill near where we lived in the hope of catching a glimpse of a satellite in the sky, which was launched by the Russians. It was called Sputnik. Despite waiting for what seemed like hours, there was no sighting of the satellite. There was a lot of discontentment and frustration on the hill with not a sight of Sputnik. The elders voiced their frustration with a litany of foul language. Well, it must have been something like that anyway, as my opening remarks to my mother when I arrived home were, 'No fuckin' Sputnik!'

Home Wasn't Built in a Day

Not long after, many satellites and rockets were launched by the Russians and Americans and everyone called them a Sputnik. Someone would often see a falling star at night only to be contradicted by someone else saying, 'Arah Jaysus, that was a Sputnik'

Sputnik was a huge phenomenon at the time. At night time, many of us would look to the skies in the hope of seeing a flickering light moving in the heavens. Our neighbours down the road, the Casey's, even called their dog Sputnik.

I'd often ask my father and mother where I came from. I always got the same answer, but it was great reassurance to hear it again and again.

'You came from Holy God, Paddy.'

That's great, I thought, since Noel Nestor told me that he was found under a head of cabbage. I must be somebody very special, coming from Holy God. Charlie Healy told me that he was found in a basket floating on the river. I thought, 'you were lucky to survive'. As far as I was concerned, there was no risk factor or chance with me, coming directly from Holy God.

My father, who was a native of Askeaton in county Limerick, was certainly not born with a silver spoon in his mouth. He was well-noted in the locality as a man who had struggled throughout his life in search of an honest penny. As a young fifteen year old, he worked in the local lime factory, known as The Mill. With his own horse and cart, he would transport bags of lime from the factory to the railway station. The Mill was a tough, uncompromising place to work. Limestone was quarried and ground into lime and then packed into eight stone bags. In his early

Paddy Cronin

days, he earned no more than a shilling a day for his efforts, which included loading and offloading the bags by hand. He had told me that one morning while carrying a load to the station, the horse collapsed and died. Not having a horse meant no wages, so after a few weeks he managed to secure the services of another horse from a local farmer which he bought for ten shillings. He paid the farmer a shilling a week from his hard earned money.

We lived in Main Street, across the road from the lime factory. This was rented accommodation, as were most houses in the village. As well as the primitive state of practically all the houses in the locality, every wall, ceiling and floor was cracked from the impact of a couple of blasts a week in the mill quarry. A loud-sounding siren would be heard for about one minute twice a week, which signalled that explosives were about to go off in the quarry. Everyone then would take to their houses until they heard the mighty blast. It shook the whole village.

As children, we saw old men with red raw eyes and white clothes leaving their shifts in the lime factory, to go home to their families, or on their way to the pub. Burned eyes and white clothes from being in constant contact with the lime. These men were hard workers who put their lives at risk to earn a living. Some of them drank a lot too – God help them, could you blame them, swallowing lime all day!

Sometimes the men would be asked to stay late to do extra work after a long hard day. They did not receive any extra payment for this. They were told if they did not want to stay late they could face the consequences and that there were plenty more outside the gate crying out for a job.

Home Wasn't Built in a Day

The quarrying and manufacture of lime brought its own hazards to the community, as windows and doors in every house were constantly covered in white dust from regular blow outs. No one complained though, as this was the main source of employment in the area. Workers at the plant worked a five-and-a-half day week. The week ended at one o'clock on Saturday. For those that had employment, it meant that hunger was kept from the door.

My parents were convinced that it was more difficult for a local to prosper than for an outsider. They put this down to a curse bestowed on the community by Saint Patrick. Legend had it that our patron Saint was walking through the town and he stopped at Mussel Lane corner on his donkey and asked for directions. A few local tricksters were there and duly made game of him and his donkey. There and then Saint Patrick put a curse on the town, saying, 'That the native may perish and the foreigner prosper.'

People in Limerick city also talked of the same curse having been bestowed on them by St. Munchin, the patron saint of the Diocese of Limerick. While building his church in Limerick in the seventh century, he asked the locals for help but was refused. Munchin was a nephew of Bloid, King of Thomond, and a Disciple of St. Patrick. Clearly this curse was handed down by Patrick, or so it was said locally.

Two landlords controlled the tenancy of all the houses in the town. One side of the street was owned by the Hunt family and the other by the Hewsons. It was said that the ownership of all these houses remained in the family of the landlords for hundreds of years. The properties had been given to them by Cromwell, on condition that they exercised English rule. As landlords, they provided you with a roof over your head, and nothing more. There was no running water and no toilet. Most households in the locality suffered the same fate. With no toilets, a bucket was used and the contents dumped in the local river. This resulted in the riverbanks being infested with rats.

Accommodation was very basic. In winter the house was damp and sometimes water would leak through the ceiling from holes in the roof. As for maintenance, this was the responsibility of the tenant. Jimmy Moran, who lived a few doors up from us, collected the rent every quarter, which amounted to £2. He was a collection agent on behalf of Hewson. If my parents did not have the money on time for the rent Jimmy Moran was always considerate, although he would stress that it was out of his hands.

On one occasion my parents told Jimmy that they were not paying the quarterly dues due to the state of the roof, which was leaking water, so he had no option but to report the non-payment to the landlord, Hewson. Hewson arrived at the house and cross words were exchanged as to the condition of the place. He agreed to make repairs once the rent was paid. The rent was paid, but no repairs were made.

Each Saturday at one o'clock an old tinkerman from the Fair Hill of Rathkeale would stand outside the exit gate of the lime plant rendering *Pal of My Cradle Days*:

Pal of my cradle days
I've needed you always
Since I was a baby upon your knee
You've sacrificed everything for me

I stroke the old gold of your hair
And I put the silver thread there
I don't know anyway I could ever repay
Pal of my cradle days

His name was 'Jimbo' Sheridan. Everybody knew 'Jimbo'. He was a decent man. As the workers left the lime plant and 'Jimbo' rendered his song, each and every one put a few coppers into his outstretched cap. 'Jimbo' led a very simple life, never indulging in any type of luxury, never drinking a drop of alcohol. After leaving the mill gates 'Jimbo' would go to the square and start to yodel which would attract every youngster in the locality. This was a very new and unique type of singing. It was very much the old man's way of rejoicing at his earnings.

I went across to Switzerland where all the Yodellers be
To try to learn to yodel and go yodel-ay-hee-dee
I climbed a big high mountain on a clear and sunny day
And there I met a young Swiss girl up in a Swiss chalet

Then we would all join in

She taught me how to yodel-----(yodel)
She taught me how to yodel-----(yodel)

Some years later, when old 'Jimbo' passed away, it was said that £30,000 was found under his mattress. I guess 'twas worth his while coming to Askeaton each Saturday morning!

Down the road from our house in Mussel Lane lived a big strong man called Mike Brien. He had a very small little house. It was just one room about ten feet by ten. The little

Paddy Cronin

house had a galvanised roof and when Mike would arrive home from the pub at night after more than a few pints he would hit the roof with his fist, as if it were a drum, proclaiming, 'It isn't a house I own, but a band'.

Mike's love for the bottle cost him his wife and four children. One morning he got up to find a note on the table from his wife, saying that she and the children had emigrated to America. They were unable to cope with his heavy drinking and being on the bread line. He never laid eyes on them again.

When de Valera was first elected Taoiseach in 1937, it was deemed that the prophesy of Saint Columcille had been fulfilled. The locals said that Columcille had prophecied that when Ireland got its real leader, a man would ride over the town bridge on a white horse. Anxious to fulfil the prophecy, Mike Brien who was a horse trader, rode over the bridge on a white stallion. Many people had gathered to witness the occasion. The crowd was then addressed in the square by old Michaelin Sheahan. Michaelin and Mike Brien got drunk as asses and on their way home, peed up against an old doorway. Both men were subsequently arrested by the Guards and charged with public order offences. They appeared at the local court and the Judge said, 'Well Mr. Brien you seem to be the ringleader, so what do you have to say for yourself?'

Mike Brien replied, 'your Honour, all I've got to say is 'Seca Jora Dora Mora.'

This was of course a cute make-up on behalf of Brien.

'What does that mean?' said the Judge.

Brien replied 'It means, your Honour, that a worthy Leader has been elected.'

Home Wasn't Built in a Day

He was referring of course to de Valera.

'Oh, I know what you are trying to say,' said the Judge, 'I certainly agree that a new era in Irish politics has begun, but I think that we have to be a little demure when celebrating such a great occasion. I hereby bind both of you to the peace for six months. I will not fine or sentence you on this occasion, taking into account the milestone you were celebrating. However, in future, please do refrain from urinating in public.'

It was obvious that the judge was an ardent follower of de Valera. Then Michaelin turned to Brien and said

'What does all this mean?'

Brien replied, 'he said, hold your piss in future!'

Michaelin Sheahan was a cousin of my father and a friend of the family. He was well known to stand at the street corner after a few whiskeys and give a speech on behalf of Fianna Fáil and Eamon de Valera. He was also a part-time bookmaker in his day. On one particular occasion, he stood at a racecourse and quoted a price of five to one on the favourite. The rest of the bookies had the same horse at even money. Michaelin took in a lot of money on the horse. Fortunately the horse lost so he did not have to pay out. One punter remarked to him, 'Well at least you gave us a good run for our money.'

Michaelin replied, 'If he'd won, I'd have given you a better run!'

During another race meeting Michaelin had a clerk informing him of the progress of a race. The clerk was my mother's brother, uncle Mikie. Mikie was watching the race through binoculars and informing him of the state of play. Again, the favourite was quoted and backed by the punters with Michaelin giving very generous odds. This time though, the favourite was running away with the race. Mikie's commentary back to Michaelin in a very low muffled voice was, 'Down with umbrella; close bag; find opening in crowd; and run.'

In anticipation of the favourite winning the race, Michaelin vacated the racecourse before the race had finished. This was very much his last hurrah as a bookmaker. The favourite had won, he had run, and the racing authorities revoked his licence forever.

Throughout the 1940s and '50s, my father would travel the length and breadth of county Limerick, to as far away as parts of county Cork showing films at local halls. This was his main source of income now, as work at the lime factory had ceased. This was mainly due to the fact that the lime was now being transported from the factory to its destination by haulage trucks. Gone were the days of delivering the bags to the railway station and loading them on to the train for despatch up and down the country. These were very tough times in Ireland, with very little employment and many emigrating to England and beyond.

My father had a little van in which he used to carry bits and pieces of equipment, like a projector and reels of film. He acquired the projector from his first cousin, Jimmy O'Brien in Limerick. Jimmy was a projectionist at the Lyric cinema and my father was able to buy it at a very reduced price, as it was an old one that they were no longer using. I often travelled with him on a Friday night to the railway station in Limerick to collect the reel of film which would arrive on the train from Dublin. Also,

Home Wasn't Built in a Day

there would be a note announcing the film which would be sent the following week. Once home, he would print the name of the following week's film on a large sheet of paper to display at the halls where he was showing the films.

Droves of people would arrive at local town halls to view the films. He would show films in our village in a shed that was owned by my mother's sisters. Before our town hall was built in the early 1950s, this was the main theatre for films, plays and travelling shows. The place would be thronged with every man, woman and child watching cowboy and Indians. One would often hear the shout, 'Oh holy Christ he's dead,' referring to someone who had been killed in the movie. The films were very real for most people and the Saturday night outing was the highlight of their week.

One night in Churchtown in County Cork, after about half an hour into a film, the projector broke down. Everyone demanded their money back. So my father proceeded to reimburse all the patrons only to run out of money before all was handed back. It seemed that a nice few people had had slipped in without paying.

One man came up though and paid the balance on behalf of my father. He said, 'If we don't cover this man, we will never see him again and it will be our loss with no pictures in the hall.'

Keeping the little van on the road was expensive in itself and my father would constantly complain about the viability of showing the pictures. My mother would often say to him, 'It makes a few bob for us, otherwise you could end up at the back of Shaws.'

Shaws was one of the big bacon factories in Limerick city. Limerick was the home of bacon and ham. People may not have had much money, but those that raised a pig and somehow managed to feed it were guaranteed a few pound when it was ready for the slaughter house. O'Mara's and Shaw's seemed to be the two big bacon houses in Limerick city. Behind Shaws there were two institutional buildings. One was the jail and the other the mental hospital. I'm not sure which one my mother was referring to, but even to me, as a small boy, neither sounded good.

TWO

I was only four years old when my father took the boat to Holyhead and then to London. On a cold and damp February morning, the sad parting took place. This was an option that wasn't taken lightly, but with very little employment available at home, emigration was the only option open to my father.

'I'm off, Bridgie, and when I get that job in London that my brother Patjoe has promised me, I will send you on the fare so that you and the children can join me.'

He had the look of a broken man. We had the look of a broken family. My mother cried bitterly as she held my sister Breda, who was just a baby in her arms. My father, who was also crying, hugged me and my sister Mary who was only about two. He cuddled my mother and the baby and vowed that things could only get better. He held an old grey suitcase in his hand. God knows what was in it. There wasn't very much to carry.

'When will you be home again Dada?' I said

He couldn't talk; his eyes were full; parting was his worst nightmare.

'When Dada?'

Then he said, 'Soon you'll be living with me in England.'

'I don't want to go to England,' I cried. 'I want us all to live at home.'

He laid the suitcase down and wiped away the tears. He hugged us all again. He made many more attempts to leave, but I clung on to his coat. Then the car pulled up at the door. I knew the parting was near. He didn't say another word. My mother ran out to the back yard. The whole situation was too much for her. He sat into the car but never looked out at us. He was broken-hearted. My mother came back in and immediately had us all join in a Hail Mary for our father. She lit a candle and said that it would guide him on his way.

My father got the job in London, but when push came to shove my mother refused to go. The furthest my mother had ever ventured was to Limerick City and that was on very few occasions, so the thought of making a new life in London was probably never on. As times became even tougher, she often regretted her decision to remain at home.

My father worked with United Dairies at Hanger Lane in Ealing. They were a big milk-producing company and they delivered bottles of milk from door-to-door all over the capital. His work was loading up the trucks for early morning delivery which meant starting at four am each morning. He was a man that was never afraid of work, so the early start was no bother to him.

My mother would often say, 'We should have gone to England with your father, they've all done well, those who have gone over there.'

Being away from his family broke my father's heart. Many a night he cried himself to sleep and dreamt of the

Home Wasn't Built in a Day

day that he would be reunited with us all and be able to support us from home. The one bright light was that he was able to send home the few bob each week and no matter how the financial situation was in the past, things were improving. Every week without fail the letter would arrive from England with a couple of English notes.

My mother was thrifty and as well as keeping the food on the table she was able to put a bit to one side. On the advice of my father my mother decided to open a sweet shop. With unemployment rife, the sweet shop barely justified its doors being open. In the shop we mainly sold sweets, penny bars, black jacks and every child's favourite, lucky bags. Fifty lucky bags came in a box and each bag contained a small toy. However, one bag also had a lucky number inside and when someone got this they won a special prize. This was usually a larger toy. My mother would always be hoping that the big prize would not be won 'til most of the box of fifty were sold. Nobody wanted to buy a lucky bag if the big prize was already won.

We also sold ice cream. The ice cream was cut from a block and sold well. It was well recognised that my mother was very generous when cutting the ice cream. As three young children, we would take our fair share of sweets from the shop. My mother found it very difficult to keep an eye on us all the time. This of course was also eating into the profits.

She would often scare us off from the sweets by saying, 'I know a family who had a shop and the children ate lots of the sweets which made them very ill with TB.' 'And what happened then Mama,' we'd say. 'They ended up in the sanatorium in Kilkenny.'

Paddy Cronin

I would worry when she'd say this, as tuberculosis was endemic at the time and we had been told at school of its dangers. Many families were touched by this disease. Those affected by it, usually ended up in a sanatorium, which was often located far away from home. People spent many years being treated in these hospitals. The story did scare us, so we tried hard to stay away from the sweets.

The stock in the shop was given to my mother on a weekly account from travellers that would call. It was important to have good sales, otherwise you would not meet the weekly instalments. Two different sweet travellers would call on a weekly basis. Jack Sidman from Limerick would call on a Monday morning. He would supply bars of chocolate and penny bars. If my mother did not have enough money to cover last week's supply, he would hold off and tell her to pay the following week. He was a generous understanding man. Another man, Mr. Moore would call on a Sunday night. He would supply the shop with cream chocolate cones. He was also very aware of our financial limitations and gave my mother every chance possible. My mother used to say that he came from a family that was once well off.

'They won the sweep at one time, but they say 'twas drank.'

The money continued to arrive each week from my father in England and it helped enormously. For the children, a parcel would arrive once a fortnight. We always waited with great excitement for the parcel. I couldn't wait to open the large box which always contained Sugar Puffs. Sugar Puffs, I thought were an English breakfast cereal. In hindsight, the reason I had not seen or heard

Home Wasn't Built in a Day

of them until my father went to England was that we simply could not afford them. Breakfast cereals were very much considered a luxury item at the time – well, to the majority of people, anyway.

Once a week, my father would phone us at the little telephone kiosk in the square. That telephone kiosk served the whole village. Who needed a phone at home anyway? Well, only if you had a loved one across the water and God knows, that scenario was becoming ever so frequent, with the possibility of earning a crust at home diminishing by the day. MacKnight's across the road from us were the only people in the street and maybe in the entire village to have a private phone. They were funeral undertakers and they needed a phone to ring through deaths to the obituary section of the national papers.

We would ring the local Post Office from the kiosk to let Mrs Roach, the Post Mistress know that we were there and waiting for my father's call. My task each week was to twist the handle on the phone before my mother picked it up to talk to Mrs Roach. The phone would ring back, 'Is that Askeaton 11?'

'Yes, Mrs Roach,' my mother would say.

'Johnny is on the line now from England'

I would immediately grab the phone.

'Hello, Dada,'

'I love you, Pat,'

'I love you too, Dada,'

'Give my love to Mary and Breda,'

'Send me a football, Dada,'

'I will go out tomorrow and buy you one.'

I couldn't wait to get the ball, nothing else seemed to

matter. The fact that he was far away in England suddenly was a sort of bonus, as I was now getting something that I probably would not have got if he was still at home. I was missing him a lot, but this was some compensation for my loss. I guess it worked the same way for him too, as, no doubt, he was missing home. I always felt that the conversations between us at home and my father at the other end of the phone were stilted and very difficult. We were not used to using a phone and it was strange talking to someone you could not see. It was a kind of yes and no dialogue.

One of the biggest events in the community, probably only second to Christmas, was the annual Point-to-Point horse racing. The races were held in early February. This was near the time of my birthday and my father sent a half-crown from England so that I could go and enjoy the day out. Chris Brandon, the harness maker from the quay was entrusted with me for the day at the races.

On race day, the community almost came to a stand still. Schools were given a day off and farmers who delivered their milk to the creamery came home early. An old man would stand at the corner near our house playing an accordion and people on their way to the races would put a few coppers in his hat.

I wasn't very concerned about what went on at the actual races, except to enjoy the many stalls selling candy floss, sweets and hand-held windmills. Every child would buy a windmill and hold it up high on the way home. A big novelty was a man from Limerick selling tickets which were placed inside a straw. The tickets were one penny each and if your number came up you won two shillings.

Home Wasn't Built in a Day

A bigger attraction than even winning the money was the fact that the man selling the tickets had a monkey on his shoulder. We would all gaze for ages at the monkey. Where on earth did he get him from? I always dreamt of having a monkey for a pet. It was such an amazing creature and I was completely fascinated by it.

These were tough times, especially for my mother, with three very young children to rear, rent to pay, and a husband in England. It was helpful though that my father was able to send home a few bob each week. The one single thing that gave her hope was her deep sense of religion. She prayed with such intensity that it was inevitably bestowed upon us. We were all brought up with the strictest religious code of conduct. Religion was always to the forefront at home. We were very traditional Irish Catholics. Mass, the Priest and prayer were first in our household. There was a Holy Water font near the front door and every time that any one of us entered or left the house, we were required to bless ourselves.

She would always remind us, 'Go nowhere without the Holy Water, 'twill protect and mind you wherever you go.'

When describing her lack of an extra few shillings, Mama would often say 'We may not be able to afford a jacket for a gooseberry but we always have God and our Faith.'

Each night before we went to bed my mother would have us kneel by the bedside and pray. Firstly we would all say the Hail Mary together and then each of us would pray to our Guardian Angel.

Angel of God, my guardian dear,
to whom God's love commits me here;

*ever this day be at my side,
to light and guard, to rule and guide. Amen.*

Our final prayer was always for the little souls in Limbo.

'Where's Limbo, Ma?' we'd often say.

'That's where little babies go if they die without being baptised,' she'd say.

'And when do they go to heaven?'

'Never, but they will always be happy there.'

'And we also pray for the souls in Purgatory?'

'Yeah,' she'd say. 'They are the souls awaiting the light of God, not fit to go to Heaven yet. It is known as a place or state of rest.'

Lotta places out there, I thought, safest bet though is to be good and go straight to Heaven! Mind you, my irreverence often brought the wrath of our mother upon me when we recited the Rosary once a week.

Friday night was Rosary night and I suppose, with school over for the week, I was full of mischievousness and up for a bit of devilment. After three or four decades, extreme boredom would set in and I would attempt to bring a little bit of light heartedness to the ritual. My mother would always give out the first part of the Hail Mary and in turn us children would answer the second part. When it would come to my turn my mother would recite:

'Hail Mary full of Grace, the Lord is with Thee, Blessed art Thou among Women and Blessed is the Fruit of Thy womb, Jesus.'

I would then answer with, 'Holy Mary Mother of God, pray for my mother, she's gone to the bog.'

This would result in my two sisters bursting into

Home Wasn't Built in a Day

uncontrollable laughter which would anger my mother greatly; well I think she may have pretended to be angry. Sarcastically she would then say to me;

'Now that's a fine example to your two young sisters alright!'

My mother's parting words before we went to bed would be, 'Cleanliness is next to Godliness.'

This ensured that we all had washed and been scrubbed in that dreaded enamel bath, with water she had brought by bucket from the public fountain in the square. Everyone used the fountain. It was the only source of fresh water. Often we would have to queue to fill our buckets. Water was also brought from the fountain to wash our clothes. My mother would wash our clothes on a washing board laid in a basin of water. God, it looked hard work as she rubbed and scrubbed the clothes against the rimmed notches of the board.

Saturday night was always the big washing night. One by one, all three of us were put in to the enamel bath and scrubbed down. That was hard enough for us to endure, but the worst was yet to come. The dreaded fine tooth comb would then appear and all three of us would beg to go last. My mother would fine comb our hair for head lice and it was a very sore procedure.

'Please Mama, I'm fine'

'I still have to check you out' she'd say.

The thoughts alone of that dreaded comb would make us shiver. That woman was determined to find every louse that pitched on our head. The unfortunate truth was that she always managed to find some.

'Where do they come from Ma?' we'd ask.

'Probably school,' she'd say.

Worse still, we would often scratch and rub ourselves against the nearest door post. We weren't alone. Everyone at school was scratching. These were the infamous fleas. I think everyone was riddled with the bloody yokes. My mother said that they came from animals, especially dogs. She also said that they came from the turf that was brought from the bog. Old men from the bogs near the Kerry border would often bring bags of turf to the village and sell them to the locals – well, to those that could afford them. I think that it must have been much cheaper to keep the fire going with turf rather than with coal as everyone seemed to have a turf fire and lots of fleas too.

We were always woken up at what seemed like an unearthly hour on Sundays. From seven o'clock the pounding of cleavers would echo throughout the house. That was Paddy Mart Sheahan, the local butcher, who had his stall a few doors down from us, preparing his meat for the customers on their way from First Mass. If Paddy Mart's cleavering did not wake us, we had no escape from Johnny Sullivan's singing at the top of his voice. Johnny would be on his donkey and cart delivering milk door-to-door for Kennedy's shop.

My mother would be up at this time, usually brushing the footpath outside the front door, littered from sweet papers and fag boxes from late night revellers from the previous night.

After Mass on a Sunday morning, my mother would give me a shilling to go to Paddy Mart's for a half a pigs head.

'A half a head, Paddy' I would say,

'Good man yourself, young Cronin.'

'I'll leave the eye in' he'd say with a chuckle, 'twill see you through the week.'

Sometimes he would throw in two mutton chops as a free extra treat. I would then run home with the half a head and the chops. Thinking that my mother would be overjoyed and delighted with the couple of extra chops, she would not show very much emotion, except to say, 'Shur Paddy Mart is all right.'

I guess pride played a big part in her emotions. I'm sure she was every bit as delighted as I was with the two chops.

At times when I would go down to Paddy Mart's stall he would call me 'Blames.'

I would ask my mother, 'Who's Blames, Mama?'

'Oh, he was a first cousin of Paddy Mart.'

'Was he famous?'

'You could say that.'

She then proceeded to tell me his story. A young couple asked Blames to drive them to the railway station in Ballingrane, which was about four miles away. They were going to Queenstown and on to America. Blames duly obliged and took them in his ass and cart.

On arrival at the railway station in Ballingrane Blames decided to go to America too. He abandoned the ass and travelled on the train to Queenstown. From there he sent a telegram to his wife. It read, 'Ass in Ballingrane, Blames in Queenstown.'

I knew then why he called me Blames. It was that he hadn't seen me in a few weeks. Pigs head was a very popular Sunday dinner. It was cheap and there was plenty of meat. My favourite part to eat was the ear. My mother would always ensure that I was the one who got the ear.

Paddy Cronin

About once a fortnight Paddy Mart would seek the help of about four men. He would stand at the front door of his butchers stall and look for a few strong men to hold a rope. This rope was attached to cows head at the back of the shop. Then you would hear the shout,

'One, two, three, right lads.'

And the men would pull as if they were in a tug-of-war. Paddy would then axe the cow until he was dead. We often watched from a little peep-hole at the side of the slaughter house and Paddy would often miss the cow's head. Sometimes it took a lot of blows before the poor animal was downed. The blood would then flow from the yard right down the street and into a gully. Hungry dogs from every nook and cranny would swarm the place and lick the blood from the roadway. The place was always stained and smelt terrible. Worse still, the slaughtered cows were skinned and left in the yard for weeks before being removed and taken to the knackers yard. God, did they smell!

I was always wishing that Paddy would choose me as one of the guys to pull the rope. I guess I'd be a man then. The call never came, though. Sheep were also slaughtered in the yard and Paddy would sometimes keep their blood in a can. He would keep it for Mick Enright, who lived up the lane. Mick would drink the blood.

'I find that it's good for me, there's nourishment in it,' he would say.

'Twas fascinating on a Sunday morning seeing the same fifteen or twenty men gathered at the old derelict house up the road from us. That place was known as Mack's Cowl. There they played 'pitch and toss.' This was a serious game and children weren't allowed near the place.

Home Wasn't Built in a Day

We had a little hideaway where we could view proceedings and nobody could see us. A stick was stuck into the ground and a circle was drawn in the mud around it. Each player in turn threw a coin to the stick. Whoever was nearest to the stick would toss two coins first. Two pennies were placed on a comb with the tail side up. They were then tossed upwards and if they didn't land on the ground heads up, the person who was second nearest the stick got the next toss. Whoever was tossing the coins and if they landed heads up, he collected all the pool of money in the circle.

One story was rumoured that a man had a penny with two heads. He apparently had won a lot of money. Another man it was said had lost a farm of land. Lots of arguments took place between the men, with many fist fights and allegations of cheating. The Guards kept a close watch on the place as pitch and toss was illegal. Often you would see Guard Kelly arrive and the group of gamblers would scamper off.

Each Sunday night at seven o'clock we would listen to the Rosary being recited at Mick Daly's. The front door of the house was forever open, so the whole street would hear the ritual. Mrs. Daly would summon all the family to take part. Apart from the religious occasion that it was, it was also a very funny event.

'Daly, come in we're sayin' the Rosary,' she would say to her husband, Mick, who would be sitting at the front door puffing his pipe.

'In the Name of the Father, Son and Holy Ghost Amen. Paddy will you put that comic out of your hand. Jaysus, Daly will you come in, we're sayin' the Rosary. Hail Mary – Oh, Jaysus! what am I sayin' at all? Dan will you stop doin' that. I'll start again. In the name . . . Jaysus, where am I? Ye have me all confused.'

It must have been the longest Rosary ever recited.

My father, in his time, would probably disagree that Daly's Rosary was the longest. Like most houses at the time, the Rosary was recited regularly. At night, his family would all go on their knees, and after the Rosary was said, my granny would have everyone say a special prayer for absent family members. With employment as scarce as it was, most of the family had emigrated to London, so the amount of prayers in addition to the Rosary was increasing by the week. My father and his sister, aunty Nancy, were eventually the only two left at home. They were none too happy with the prayer ritual and one evening my father turned to Nancy and said, 'For God's sake, please stay at home, 'cause if one more leaves home I'll be on my knees for the whole bloody night!'

In between the Rosary at Daly's, you'd often hear the loud grunting of a boar pig. Casey's on the bridge kept a boar to service all the sows in the locality. Every young child in the area had a reasonable understanding of the facts of life, courtesy of Casey's boar and the visiting sows. We would often hear the commotion at the top of the street.

'Go on, go on, go on aur dat, go on'

This usually was Mike Kenneally guiding one of his fat sows down to the Casey's yard for a service. Lots of the local children would run down to view the proceedings.

'Get away aur dat, get home to yer mother,' John Joe Casey would shout.

The show was too good for us to take John Joe Casey's advice. We would hide in the trees beside the yard and watch the proceedings. This was sex education at its absolute best.

While my father was in England, my mother's brother Mikie stayed with us. Mikie never married and my mother took care of him lovingly. He worked as a labourer in the building of a runway at Shannon Airport or Rynanna, as it was then known. Lots of men from the locality worked in Rynanna. It was one of the very few jobs available, although much of the time the work was on a part time basis. At school, we even learned a new rhyme about the airport. Mind you, 'twas in the school yard rather than in the classroom that we learned the short verse.

There was an old man from Rynanna
Who thought he could play the piano,
The piano slipped, his trousers ripped,
And next there was a banana.

We were in big trouble if we recited that verse at home. My mother would rage at us.

'Where did ye hear that?' she'd say.

'I don't know Mama,' we'd say.

'Cut out that filth, ye'll bring the wrath of God down on us,' she'd say.

Mikie would travel to and from Rynanna each day. A man up the road from us, known as the 'Mixer' Murphy also worked there. He had a van and he would bring a crew of workers to and from Shannon each day, Uncle Mikie being one of them.

Every Friday without fail, Mikie would give my mother a ten shilling note from his wages. I couldn't wait for him to open his wage packet so that I could have the empty envelope. The envelope was made of brown paper with a plastic window. We had never seen plastic before. He also told us that similar plastic was being put underneath the new runway at the airport.

'What's it for?' we'd ask.

'I suppose it prevents the dampness coming up through the surface,' he'd say.

I'd keep loads of the wage packets so that I could show the plastic to my friends at school. They were all fascinated with this window-like paper. The teacher even displayed it in class. I was so proud to be part of this new invention, plastic.

We all loved it when Mikie brought home the crubeens from Limerick. These were little pigs trotters. Mama would boil them and usually there would be enough for one each. She would say, 'Eat them up. There's plenty of fat in them; ye'll need it for the winter.'

Less and less work became available at Shannon and my father tried to persuade Mikie to join him in England. In August 1958 he invited him to London, where he promised to fix him up with a job. Mikie though was not very interested in going across the water, but with some gentle persuasion by my mother he decided to give it a try. However, it became an even bigger struggle for my father to persuade Mikie to remain in London, as he became very homesick. He returned home to us in early October, spending a mere two months in London. My father continued to work in England and returned home in mid-December. However, his stay was a short one, as he had to return to work sooner than expected. Nevertheless, we had a happy time together. He did show a desire to remain at

Home Wasn't Built in a Day

home and inquired about possible jobs in the locality, but he was met with the same answer all round.

'There's little for anybody round here.'

Day after day he went out in search of a job, but had no luck at all.

He used to tell us great stories about London,

'I go up to Hyde Park Corner every Sunday morning and listen to every Godforsaken man talk about everything under the sun,' he'd say. 'There are trains that travel underground and great big double-decker buses to take you the length and breadth of the city.'

I guess he was painting a nice picture of London, in the hope that we would join him there.

The ports were getting even busier with many more people taking the boat to England. It was clearly evident throughout the community that there were less and less men to be seen. Entire families too, decided to go in search of a better life. Christmas arrived, and Santa Claus did arrive as usual with me getting the promised motor car, Mary the doll and pram and Breda a little teddy bear. After Christmas, my father returned to England and this time it happened without any of us children realising it. I had come to understand and accept that he would be spending a lot of time away from home. I suppose I was not altogether alone as a few more in my class at school had fathers away too. I just returned home from school one evening to find out that he had gone back. I'm sure that the date was well planned, but neither he nor my mother wanted a formal parting from us children.

I asked my mother where my father was and her answer was, 'He'll be back before you know it.'

THREE

August 1959 was a memorable time for me, not least coming face-to-face with a helicopter for the first time. Commotion hit the community and indeed the entire city and county with the news that Todds department store in Limerick city had been burnt down. Todds was an institution. It was reputed to have sold everything from a 'needle to an anchor.'

As children, we always associated Todds with Santa Claus as the great man would be there each Christmas. Our parents always ensured that we visited Santa in Todds every year, and somehow they always managed to afford this, seeing it as part of their parental duty.

It was said at the time of the fire that over one million pounds worth of damage was done to the store. Lipton's General Store, next door to Todds was also destroyed. Young men climbed the hundred foot ruined castle across the road from our house where they could see the raging flames of the towering inferno. This was incredible as Limerick city, where the fire was, was sixteen miles away.

The Sheehy Brothers, who were a well-known firm of demolition contractors, were hired for the salvage and clean-up operation. They were from our village of

Home Wasn't Built in a Day

Askeaton. As part of the final demolition, a helicopter was used with a ball and chain suspended from it to knock the shell to the ground. The Sheehys hired the helicopter from a company in Hampshire, in England. To everyone's amazement and excitement they brought the helicopter to their native Askeaton after the clean-up and final demolition of Todd's was completed.

Every man, woman and child from the village came to see the landing of this amazing machine. They landed in a field across from the Protestant church. They then offered to bring people on a flying tour of the locality. Loads of people took to the skies. My uncle Mikie brought me there, but was too protective of me and wouldn't allow me to go up in the helicopter. He said that it was too dangerous for me, but I guess he was too nervous to go up himself. I was the perfect excuse for him not venturing to the skies.

With my father in England, Mikie took care of me as if I was his own son. He would sometimes call me out of bed at two or three o'clock in the morning to listen to a Floyd Patterson fight on the wireless. He would take ages to tune the wireless into the station it was broadcast on. Eventually after slow movements of the wireless knob, he would hit upon the channel. Patterson was world heavyweight boxing champion. Mikie would re-enact every punch and every move of Patterson. His arms and hands would fly in all directions.

'Go one Patterson, give it to him; go on you beauty.'

Mikie would also teach me old rhymes and riddles and took great pride when I would reel them off to him again. He would often take me to our front door and stop a passer by and say, 'Listen to this. Go on, Paddy, say the poem' I would proceed to recite one of his favourite rhymes that he had taught me;

> *Baa baa black sheep, have you any wool?*
> *Yes sir, yes sir, three bags full!*
> *One for the master, one for the dame,*
> *And one for the little boy who lives down the lane.*

He was so proud to hear me. He also had me convinced that I was the little boy who lived down the lane. Great, I thought, to have a poem written about me. Mikie was a great singer and often would come home at night and entertain us all. One of his favourite songs was 'The Juice of the Barley.'

> *In the sweet County Limerick, one cold winter's night*
> *All the turf fires were burning when I first saw the light;*
> *And a drunken old midwife went tipsy with joy*
> *As she danced round the floor with her slip of a boy,*
>
> *Singing ban-ya-na mo if an-ga-na*
> *And the juice of the barley for me.*
>
> *Well when I was a gossoon of eight years old or so*
> *With me turf and me primer to school I did go.*
> *To a dusty old school house without any door,*
> *Where lay the school master blind drunk on the floor*

Time passed quickly and before we knew it, we were looking forward to Christmas once again and the return of my father. He arrived back home for Christmas in early December 1959 and decided to convert the sweet shop into a toy shop. The house was filled with excitement on the announcement of his homecoming. He took the

Home Wasn't Built in a Day

boat from Holyhead to Dublin and then the train on to Limerick. I became ill with measles some days before his arrival, which resulted in me being in bed when he landed back home. He immediately ran upstairs to the bedroom, burst into an unstoppable fit of crying and hugged me for what seemed an eternity, saying, 'I love you, I love you.'

He cuddled my two sisters and did not want to let go of them, as if he was afraid they did not remember him. The most precious moment to him was having his wife and three children around him again. He then promised us all that Santa would bring us something nice as he had written to him while he was in England. He asked me what I wanted from Santa and to his astonishment I said, 'I want a pair of glasses, I find it very hard to see.'

There was nothing whatsoever wrong with my eyesight but one of the lads at school had just got a pair of glasses and I definitely wanted them too.

'OK,' said my father 'we must test your eyes first.'

He then put a fly into a milk bottle, asked me to hold the bottle up to the light, look into the bottle and tell him if I could see the fly. I could see the fly and immediately said, 'Yes'.

I was fearful that the fly would fly out and into my eye. That was the end of the glasses for Christmas! My two sisters were probably too young to understand the significance of my father's return. Mary was only three years old and Breda only two. They nevertheless knew that the homecoming was a major event. At last we were a proper family again, in that we were all together. It was a wonderful feeling to get up each morning knowing that both my father and my mother were at home.

Paddy Cronin

A great warmth had now descended upon the whole family. That same Christmas my father brought much joy to the many children of the area with the presence of Santa Claus in the shop, the large number of toys on display, and especially the Triang train, which was running constantly in the front window. That train he brought back with him from England, having purchased it at Hamleys in London. Having a toy shop in a small village meant that instead of going to Limerick city, people from the locality did not have to travel far for Christmas gifts, so it was supported very well. Cronin's Toy Shop was a haven for children. Droves of children would congregate outside the window looking at the train. I was fascinated by all the toys on display.

My father said, 'Santa will call on Christmas Eve and take these toys away with him for many of the children in the locality. Some toys he cannot make himself so he picks them up here.'

I was totally chuffed that Santa had that special relationship with my father. I had told my school friends about this special relationship, but they already knew, as their own parents had told them that Santa would call to Cronin's shop on Christmas Eve to pick up some toys. Mikie bought a goose that Christmas which he brought home to my mother on Christmas Eve. He then sent me to Johnny Mulcair's shop, which was just up the road from us, for two large candles. These candles were about four foot high. Mikie then cut a hole in two turnips and wedged the candles in them. I was given the privilege of lighting the Christmas candles. Everyone knelt and prayed in front of the candles and my mother reminded

Home Wasn't Built in a Day

us that we were celebrating the birth of Jesus and that the lights were there to show the way to the Holy Family.

Not many people put a Christmas tree up for Christmas. There were lots of lighted candles though, and little cribs depicting the Holy Family. Then Mikie burst into verse with the greatest of reverence.

Silent night, holy night
All is calm, all is bright
Round yon Virgin Mother and Child
Holy Infant so tender and mild
Sleep in heavenly peace
Sleep in heavenly peace

As children Mikie's singing was a bit too formal for us so we burst into our own verse which I had learned at school and had taught to my two sisters.

Christmas is coming
And the goose is getting fat,
Please put a penny
In the old man's hat.
If you don't have a penny,
A ha'penny will do,
And if you haven't a ha'penny,
God Bless you!

Christmas Day was special! Santa arrived with presents that were opened from dawn, and most importantly, all the family were together. With *Adeste Fideles* playing aloud from the wireless and the smell of roasted goose from the range, it was one happy family celebrating a great occasion.

Paddy Cronin

Before the big bird was roasted, my mother removed the two feathered wings ever so carefully. These were used as dusters for the top of the range throughout the year. She kept them on top of the mantle piece behind the picture of Pope John XXIII whom she revered on a daily basis. The goose wings were kept there for the next twelve months.

Although there was much furore and excitement all through the house, we were not allowed to forget the real meaning of the festivities. All of us went to the First Mass of Christmas Day, which was at nine o'clock. Us children were up since six, checking out what Santa had brought, so we had awakened the whole house early. Our village resembled the Wild West of America on Christmas Day. At every corner you had cowboys and Indians. Every young lad in the locality must have got a cowboy suit and cap gun from Santa. Young fellows with cowboy hats and guns in holsters patrolled the streets. From early morning the sound of the cap guns and Wild West chatter reverberated throughout the village.

'Bang, bang your dead.'

'Giddy up, giddy up.'

Then would come the knock on the shop door, 'Mrs Cronin, I'm out of caps, so I can't use my gun. Can I have a roll of caps please?'

'Ok,' she'd say, 'just this once, 'tis Christmas day so I don't want any more of you knocking.'

'Thanks Mrs Cronin.'

But, of course, the knock came again and again, and each time my mother would answer and warn that this was the last time.

Home Wasn't Built in a Day

The toy shop proved to be a real winner during Christmas of '59 with a very decent turnover. At last, there seemed to be light at the end of the tunnel. My father decided to remain at home and make a real go of the shop, selling sweets and the odd few groceries as well as toys. We were all delighted with his decision to stay.

After Christmas and facing a long winter, things were not as rosy as they seemed at first. Money was scarce once again and spending was nearly at a standstill. Business had slackened off in the shop with only the odd person here and there buying something. Nevertheless, both my father and mother persevered, but it was a total uphill struggle. However, they both vowed to try and make it work, at least for the sake of their three children. It was important to them to keep the family unit together and for my father to return to England would only be as a last resort.

My mother would say, 'If we just keep our head above water, I'll be happy.'

The problem was that through all the honest endeavours, their struggle was becoming more intense by the day. One could always tell that my father was never far from taking that infamous boat back to England again. My mother though soldiered on, always praying that things would pick up and that the emigration route would never have to be taken again.

FOUR

It was a frosty Saturday morning in early February when my father brought local handy man, Mikie Maigner, to Limerick in his old small van. Mikie's mission in the city was to buy a gramophone record. Ferrying the odd person here and there meant an extra few shillings for my father. He was what you might call an unauthorised taxi. On many occasions he would transport a van-full of young buck bachelors to dances, which were held in other parts of the county. Young men would call at the weekends and ask to be driven up to twenty or thirty miles to a dance. This was a time when buses did not operate between towns and if one did not have their own car, they would have to cycle. Mikie Maigner wanted to be driven to Limerick to purchase John Mac Cormack's *Love Thee Dearest*. Coming home in the van, Mikie declared that he had bought six copies of the record.

'Why?' said my father, 'did you buy six of the same record?'

'Just to be sure, said Mikie, in case they run out.'

Mikie was fearful that by playing the record too often on the gramophone, it would somehow erase itself.

'You're very much into gadgets Mikie,' said my father.

Home Wasn't Built in a Day

'Well Johnny, I was the first person in Askeaton to have a wireless. I won it at a game of cards and when the man of the house ran out of money, I was given the wireless. Micheal O Hehir, the renowned Gaelic games commentator, did his first commentary in 1938 and more than a hundred people listened to the game outside my door that day.'

Old Mikie was well-known in the community, having made headlines digging his own grave and building his headstone, in preparation for the day when he would die and be laid to rest. Each day, he would go to the grave, which was in the grounds of the ruined Franciscan Abbey and empty the earth from the six-foot-deep hole. He would return at night to fill it in, fearful that somebody might fall into it in the dark. He lined the grave with red brick, deeming that red brick kept out the dampness and that dampness was bad for the bones. Mikie had a very philosophical outlook towards death; it was inevitable, so he may as well make it as comfortable as possible.

He used to sleep with his own father, only to wake one night to discover that the old man was cold as mutton, stiff as a poker and dead as a maggot. He subsequently put the father over his shoulder and brought him down the stairs and placed him on a chair in the kitchen. Mikie then went back to bed and slept through the rest of the night. The following morning he called the priest to administer the last rights.

'So he died here on the chair?' said the priest.

'No' said Mikie, 'he died up in bed.'

'And how did he get down here?' said the priest.

'I brought him down.' said Mikie, 'He was too cold to sleep beside.'

Not long after completion of his own grave, Mikie slipped on a banana skin, injured himself badly, and died a few days later. His funeral was a very dignified occasion. He had commissioned four workers from the nearby creamery as pallbearers; the Priest and the undertaker had also been paid in advance. Mikie wanted to make absolutely sure that he would have the most perfect burial ever.

Financially things seemed to improve at home, with my father securing a part-time job with the Board of Works as a jeep driver. The old van he had was on the last legs and wasn't worth taxing or insuring, so it ended up in the scrap yard. The Board of Works job was based in Bruff, which was over twenty miles away and this carried its own problems, trying to arrange transport to and fro. Many a day and night he walked miles and miles to get there or to return home. Not having his own mode of transport meant that he had to hitch a lift, which proved very difficult at times, as the volume of traffic back then was fairly insignificant. Often it would be very late before he would arrive home, exhausted from the journey.

Meanwhile, my mother had become very concerned about her brother Mikie's general health. He was not a well man and was barely able to get out of bed in the mornings. He also had what seemed to be a persistent cough that no amount of medicine would shift. She had read about a priest in Italy who had the stigmata of Christ. His name was Padre Pio. She wrote to Padre Pio asking him to pray for Mikie's welfare. Padre Pio wrote back and told her that Mikie would be fine and to put everything in the hands of God. From that day forward she became a champion of Padre Pio and after his death she promoted his name,

Home Wasn't Built in a Day

distributed his relics and prayed to him and for him for the rest of her life. If ever we were in any type of distress or if anyone else was, she would pray to Padre Pio for guidance and help. He gave her great inspiration in times when religion was very often her only comfort. She became so close to him that she called him 'My Man'. If somebody was in any sort of bother she would often say, 'I'll say a prayer to My Man for you.' As far as my mother was concerned, most of her prayers and intercessions were answered.

My father had told me of this great new invention in England called television. I could not fully understand the concept, but nevertheless it totally fascinated me. I understood that all of us would be on television. The thing was, that I thought that my mother and father could see me at school and this I saw as a major problem. I had been warned at home to stay away from certain individuals and in the main, I did. But what if we were playing a game in the school yard and those that were not considered suitable company were caught up in the game? I would then be seen in their company. Also, more importantly, I was being walked to school every day by a lady friend. Now then, I did not want that to be known. I was probably about six and I had ideas about my girlfriend Geraldine Collins. No, television was definitely not for me. I told my friends at school what my father had told me but they laughed it off.

'That could never happen,' they said. 'You're talking about the pictures they show in the Savoy cinema in Limerick.'

'There's no way you can have a cinema in your own kitchen.'

'Well, my father told me, he saw it in England. All you do is put a yoke on your chimney and you will have a picture in a box in the kitchen.'

My father also said that some people used a bicycle wheel to receive the television signal. The spokes of the wheel would attract the signal. I immediately went down to an old dump near our house and found an old bicycle wheel. I brought it home in the hope that we could have television. Unfortunately my father told me that we would need a television unit, which in our wildest dreams we could never afford. Anyhow, he said that television was only available in England. There was talk that it would soon be available in Ireland, but as usual, it would be a luxury that very few people would be able to afford, well, certainly not us anyway.

My father and mother were great to attend funerals, especially when it was a local one, when one of the natives had died. A native was someone who lived in the village and whose ancestors were born and bred there. If somebody lived outside the confines of the village, and more importantly, if their family was not native there for hundreds of years, they were classed as 'foreigners'. Chris Nash who lived down the lane had passed away. He was of 'old stock'. It was no surprise then to see my father and mother get ready to see him off to the church.

My mother then said to me; 'We are going down the lane to Nash's; Chris the old fisherman has died and we need to pay our respects.'

There was a wake at the house for Chris and many of his old drinking buddies came to pay their last respects. It was decided to shoulder the coffin from the house to the

Home Wasn't Built in a Day

church, which was about a mile away. An institution at all funerals, Charlie Madigan helped to shoulder the coffin. Charlie was always a friend of the deceased, as it meant plenty of whiskey being dished out. He was always the first to announce a death in the village. He would travel the length and breadth of the town telling every man, woman and child the news that someone had 'kicked the bucket'. He was well-known for carrying an onion in his handkerchief to induce the tears at wakes.

No matter if somebody was seriously ill or not, when asked about their well-being, Charlie's response would always be with the same pessimism, 'You can take it from me, another clane (clean) shirt will do him.'

At most funerals, Charlie was the great mourner, the chief pallbearer, the best friend of the deceased, the principal drinker of whiskey and the biggest rogue.

'Jaysus, he was my best friend,' said Madigan.

After an all night wake and lots of the finest malt whiskey, it was time to shoulder the coffin to the church. It was a great honour to shoulder a coffin all the way to the church; a privilege was only afforded to old stock such as Chris.

On the way, outside Hough's pub, Madigan shouted, 'Leave the coffin down, Chris. Have a drink on us; old stock.'

As they passed each pub, it was down with the coffin and Charlie declaring 'Have a drink on us Chris, the Lord have mercy on the Holy Souls, wherever they are.'

As they reached the church door, everyone under the coffin was exhausted. Madigan, who was small and light, tripped, and the coffin almost hit the floor. Somehow, they stopped the coffin from hitting the ground. Charlie Madigan was never seen under a coffin again after that.

Paddy Cronin

Whenever my parents went to a funeral, they would never call to a house on their way home. They would always come home first. It was deemed bad luck if you did not come straight to your own home after a funeral.

'If you go to bury the dead, let that be your mission and nothing else,' they would say.

Whenever they did not attend a funeral, which was very seldom, as in a small village like ours everyone went to everybody's funeral, and when the hearse was passing the front door, all the house lights were switched off, curtains closed and the door leading out onto the street closed. This was showing respect for the dead. Every house and business did the same. We would often be inside the window watching a funeral pass by on its way from the church to the graveyard. As children we would count the cars and horse and traps. We would immediately be told to stop by one or other of our parents, as this practice was deemed very unlucky.

We have a great custom here in Ireland of never ever saying anything bad or derogatory about the dead. If somebody passes on, we only say good things about them. Charlie Madigan was an unofficial helper to undertaker John Mac Knight and as a funeral would move slowly through the village, Charlie would always be seen seated at the passenger side of the hearse. At one particular funeral and when the cortège was about to enter the village, Charlie started foul-mouthing about the dead person in the coffin behind him.

'A lightin' bastard he was,' said Madigan.

John Mac Knight, the undertaker, was fearful of what curse or misfortune might befall him and immediately pulled up his hearse and ejected Madigan. This was Charlie's last time travelling with Mac Knight to or from a funeral.

With my father and mother trying to survive on part-time wages from the Board of Works, something else was needed to supplement the family income. My father decided to take to the road buying the contents of orchards and selling them to shops. He somehow managed to buy a small van. He sold the apples mainly in the Limerick, Clare and Kerry regions, calling to small shops and in some cases individual houses. Many youngsters from the locality were rounded up to pick the apples in local orchards. Of course, all of the young lads picking the apples had their fill and he had no objection to that. We all felt so sorry for Declan Sheahan though. Declan spent three days on the bucket after what appeared to be the consumption of over thirty apples. His mother insisted that that was the end of his apple picking. She said to my father;

'Johnny, forget about Declan in future, he never knows when to stop.'

The Sheahans lived near the bridge, with their backyard extending right onto the river Deel. Patrick, Michael, William and Declan were forever fishing out their back window. This was a huge novelty and something that we were all very envious of. They did not even need a fishing rod to capture the fish. More often than not, they would use a hand-line with a worm as bait and sometimes would leave it in the river over night. Usually this resulted in the line been stuck under a rock, courtesy of an eel. It was here that patience played a big part, because if one of the Sheahans, usually Declan, did not continue to gently

Paddy Cronin

tug away at the line and encourage the eel out, he would risk losing the hook, as eventually the line would break. Whenever the Sheahans had a hand-line out their back window, one of the boys would guard it like a hawk. There were too many pranksters around, and anyway someone already fishing outside Sheahans' back door, was never going to say no to a fresh brown trout.

Apple-picking time was from mid-August to late October. With the help of my mother we would box the apples in our kitchen and then do what was known as topping them off. The inferior apples were put lower down in the box and the more appealing ones were put on top. This helped when selling, but it also meant that sometimes you could not return to the same shop or customer for a long time – well, at least until that shopkeeper had forgotten who sold them the box of apples, half of which turned out to be either rotten or smaller in size than those that were at the top.

A sports day was advertised to take place in the hurling field in Adare on the 15th of August. My father saw this as an opportunity to sell apples at the field. Earlier in the week we had picked five or six boxes of early apples called 'Beauty of Bath' at an orchard in Ballysteen, so this was a good opportunity to sell them off. I went with him to the sports day in Adare and we set up a little stall just outside the gate. I stood there with him selling the apples and the venture was going well. Then, lo and behold, out of nowhere, came this black-clad, very irate man shouting and roaring at us to get out of Adare.

'Get out of here you intruders,' he shouted

'Why?' said my father, in a very low voice.

'Because I said so and show me your hawkers licence?' said the angry clergyman

'I have none,' said my father

'Well, off with you then,' he said

I was crying and shaking with fear. The man who had hounded us away was the local Catholic curate, Father Casey. We returned home feeling sorry for ourselves and angry at the man who had deprived us of a day's living. My mother always said that there was not an hour's luck in selling apples. Maybe she was right. She maintained that their ill fortune was derived from Adam and Eve. The first original sin was committed by Adam and Eve eating the forbidden fruit from an apple tree in the Garden of Eden. Thankfully for my mother, the apple-selling season was short enough, so the ill fortune that it brought, was also short-lived.

My father's next venture was on the road, selling fish. This was during the winter, when apples were out of season. He would buy the fish from a fishmonger in Limerick city and then travel the countryside, going from door to door. This venture never really got off the ground and only lasted for a few months. When he could not make ends meet, he gave up. Another man from a neighbouring village was selling fish at the same time, so the market was already covered. To try and discredit this other man we made up a rhyme and recited it at school and everywhere we could:

John Dillon sells fish,
Twopence ha'penny a dish,
Don't buy them, don't buy them,
They're full of cat's shit.

Paddy Cronin

In spite of all the efforts, the fish venture was doomed from the very beginning.

I accompanied my father on numerous occasions to Abbeyfeale on the Kerry border to visit the home of TD, Jimmy Collins. He was the father of the recent Government Minister and MEP, Gerry Collins. Politicians had great power in those days. They were looked up to as miracle workers. My father's visit to the Collins' household was usually on a job-hunting mission. I'm not sure if my father's petitions and Collins' representation worked in his favour or not. My father swore by Fianna Fáil and the power that its officers carried.

My mother, on the other hand, would go hungry rather than ask a Fianna Fáiller to do her a turn. She was the very opposite, a Fine Gael fanatic. She was a True Blue Shirt, a Michael Collins supporter and never denied it. The Blue Shirts, who were aligned to Fine Gael, were supported by the Catholic Church, and had aided Franco in the Spanish uprising. My father said that their founder, Eoin O'Duffy, was a fascist and was no better than Hitler himself.

My mother often boasted that, as a young girl, she painted a hen blue and let it loose through the town. This was in the lead up to a Government election. She certainly let her colours be known! She also blamed de Valera for Collins' death. My father, though, was Fianna Fáil through and through and was equally open about it. In fact, on election days they would go their separate ways to vote and never spoke for the whole day. My mother's family were Blue Shirts; they were also hackney people and on election day, they would carry Fine Gael voters to and from the Polling Booths free-of-charge.

Home Wasn't Built in a Day

Election day in town brought tension and unrest across the entire community. In many instances, friends and family were divided. Slurs and innuendos were exchanged freely among the voters. The local school became the polling station and many scuffles took place outside it. The War of Independence was never forgotten by hardened supporters on either side and this made for many bitter exchanges. The good thing was, that once the election was over, the same people who had despised each other on Polling Day sat down together, shook hands, and shared a drink thereafter. However, the peace was not maintained when de Valera came to nearby Foynes to give a speech. As he addressed the masses, he was capsized from the platform by Jack Mulqueen from Askeaton. Mulqueen had a wooden leg, and he used it as a lever to topple the stage, resulting in the Fianna Fáil leader falling to the ground.

My mother also gave us another great piece of advice, 'Never discuss politics or religion with anyone,' she would say. In truth, in this case, she never practiced what she preached, as she was a self-professed expert in her opinions on both.

FIVE

On the 7th of May 1960, I received my First Holy Communion. I wore a little short grey pants, a white shirt and red tie which had been bought for me by my very proud parents. Even though money was not plentiful they managed to bring me to Kingston's shop, in William Street, Limerick, to be fitted out for the occasion. The ritual scrubbing in that enamel bath and the fine combing of the hair took place the night before. My father had to head for Bruff where he was working, at five o'clock that morning, breaking his heart that he could not be with me on my big day. My mother called me at seven o'clock. What an unearthly hour to be up for the proudest day of my life! The reason that I was called so early, was so that my mother could find some man on his way to work to make a tie knot for me. John Culhane, on his way to the local lime factory, duly obliged.

'Will you tie a knot on Paddy's tie for him? He's making his First Communion this morning,' my mother asked John.

'O' course I will,' said John.

'And have a lovely day, my son and here's a half-a-crown to start your day.'

Home Wasn't Built in a Day

That half-crown was more than welcome, as it gave me a head start in the money stakes. The money aspect of the day was just as important as the day itself – well, for me anyway. Monday in school would no doubt be a day of collating and then boasting about the money earned by all of us children. Before we left for the church I asked my mother for a cup of water. I was nervous and had a very dry mouth. I was fasting from twelve o' clock the night before. The Church rule was that one had to fast from the night before.

'No,' she said, 'I don't think that even water is allowed.'

My mother brought me to the church that day and put me in my seat near the altar in the main isle. I was nervous, but so were the other boys and girls on their big day. After putting me in my seat, my mother went to the side aisle with my two little sisters. I'm sure she would have wished that my father could have been there too, but at least now he was back in Ireland.

After I had received my First Communion, my mother brought me to all the friends and relations to show me off in all my glory. She was so proud of her young son. It was a very happy day for everyone. I remember spending a few hours with my aunts Katie and Eileen. Katie took a photo of me with her box camera. My sisters, Mary and Breda, were not too sure what was up, or what all the fuss was about.

My father arrived home that night and I relived the excitement of the day with him, while my mother baked the usual flat cake on the griddle pan. The cake we would eat whilst still hot after supper. The biggest part of the day had now arrived. I began to count the money I made throughout the day. There were a few half-crowns, lots of shillings and a ten shilling note.

'I made £2 and 15 shillings,' I said.

'Put that away in the Post Office,' said my mother. 'Anybody who has anything today still has their First Communion money.'

I had better ideas though, like going to Woolworths in Limerick. That evening, my father brought me to see my grandmother. He was as proud as punch showing off the First Communion boy to his mother.

'You're a very smart boy, Paddy' she said to me, pushing a shiny half-crown into my hand. 'And you're a credit to your mother and father.'

I was now beginning to feel a bit embarrassed by all the attention. Still I was nearly up to £3 now, which meant my Post Office account was going to be extremely healthy.

Granny always looked on the brighter side of life; the glass was always half-full rather than half-empty. Her turn of phrase and wit was well-renowned in the locality. She was a jolly lady, whose lively demeanour drew many an interesting character to her door. Paddy Leahy would come to the village each night for a pint or two, and indeed, on his way home would not be shy to give a bar of his favourite and only song *The Rose of Tralee*. Paddy would love the applause at the end and the cheers of, 'Good boy, Leahy.'

He was a simple man, simple in the sense of being shy and unassuming. Having felt that he entertained, made him happy. Paddy spent most of his early years in Glin Industrial School. He showed a deep sense of gratitude that he had been rescued from the clutches of the terrible

Home Wasn't Built in a Day

people who had employed him in his early years. He was appreciative for have been given a second chance in life. He was an innocent and quiet soul, who personified the simple way of life and made it seem almost desirable. On one particular evening, he was passing Granny's house on his way to the pub, when she ran out and called him.

'Hey Paddy, she said, which of your legs is the longest?'

'Don't know Mrs. Cronin,' replied Paddy.

'Well,' said Granny, 'between them it is then, Paddy'

'I suppose you're right Mrs. Cronin' said Leahy.

Paddy Leahy was a servant boy who had been employed by a variety of farmers since leaving Glin Industrial school in the 1920s. The poor old devil told me of his early days at Glin, where he had the cat-of-nine-tails used on him. Glin Industrial school was operated by The Christian Brothers, who ran it with the help of state funding. If parents simply lacked a steady income, or if they broke up, or if a birth was out of wedlock the so-called 'cruelty men' would come to take the children away to Glin. Children who had committed crime, no matter how small, or children who were destitute, neglected, orphaned or abandoned, were sent to an Industrial school. Paddy never spoke about his mother or father. I doubt if he ever even knew them.

Terrible and fearful stories emerged from Glin. The fear of Glin Industrial School hung over every young person, and ensured that you were always well-behaved. If anyone stepped out of line, Glin was a very real option. Well, we thought that anyway. My mother would often threaten me with Glin if I was misbehaving.

My sisters also had the threat of another institution hanging over them. Not Glin though, as this was a boys only reformatory. The institute for their misdemeanours would be the Mount convent in Limerick city. The threat alone was enough to keep all of us in line. Every mother and father of the time used the same tactic.

We were all horrified to hear of a terrible story about an Industrial school in Donegal. Eight girls tried to escape the school but were caught and had their heads shaved by the nuns. Around the same time, a little boy at the Glin school had his face badly beaten by a Christian brother. He ended up in the Limerick Regional Hospital. Another young boy there was flogged naked with the cat-of-nine-tails and immersed in salt water for trying to escape to see his mother. The authorities seemed to never blink an eye at all the horrible stories, as all these punishments and beatings were expected if you were unfortunate enough to be confined to an Industrial school. Conditions at Glin were terrible for the children; the building was cold and draughty and only two paltry meals were served each day, morning and evening. All the terrible stories frightened the livin' daylights out of us. An adult Paddy Leahy recounted his own story to me:

'After leaving Glin Industrial School at the age of fifteen, I was fostered out to a farmer near Athea, in West Limerick. After many a hard day out on the farm, picking potatoes, I would come in to the farmer's house only to be given a mug of tea and a slice of bread. That farmer often beat me with the belt he had around his waist. The man that brought me here to Askeaton, though, gave me a much better life and I am thankful to him for that.'

Granny had loads of funny stories to tell. One that comes to mind is about Chris Brandon, who was the local harness-maker, who lived on the Quay beside her. Chris was a man that me and many of my friends were on the run from. Every time that any of us passed his door we would shout 'leather belly' in at him. I suppose we called him leather belly because he had leather hanging all over his shop, which he used in his trade. He would then follow us like a madman down the Quay, until our young legs got the better of him. Chris's sister, Lizzy, had an operation in Limerick Regional hospital and he called to Granny to inform her as to how she was after the ordeal.

'She's fine,' said Chris, 'and over the operation, and to tell you the truth, it made a man of her.'

My grandmother, who thought this was absolutely hilarious, went straight for Jim Ryan who worked next door to her house. She declared to Jim, 'Lizzy Brandon's operation was not all that straightforward after all.

'Why?' said Jim.

'Whatever they've done to her now, it's made a man of her, and that's serious!'

The Saturday after my First Communion, my father finished work around midday and, as a treat, he brought me to Woolworths in Limerick. Going to Limerick city was always a very big day out for a country boy. Woolworths was where every young lad dreamed of visiting. My father bought me a jar of bubbles which I blew all day. Bubbles were a huge novelty. Somehow blowing bubbles was a sign that you had been to the city. He also bought me a small yellow plastic pipe. My father was a smoker and as he would come to the end of his cigarette he would put the butt in my pipe for me to smoke. I must have smoked dozens of Gold Flake fag butts by the time I was just six or seven! Of course, in those days, cigarettes were widely known to be good for you!

No trip to Limerick would be complete without a visit to the butcher for a bag of tripe. Once home, my mother would cook the tripe with onions and we would eat it the following day. Once the tripe and onions were cooked, it was always best to leave them in the pot overnight to marinate. I can still smell that unique aroma throughout the house once she cooked our favourite dish.

Whenever my father would open a new packet of cigarettes, I would ask him for the silver paper which surrounded the top of the Gold Flake packet. I would then take the silver paper to school. Every child brought silver paper to school. Some brought in more than others. If one of your parents smoked Gold Flake, Players or Sweet Afton, you were fine, as these packets contained the silver paper. Now, if they smoked Woodbine, you were in trouble, as the Woodbine pack did not have the proper paper. It had a kind of silver with a paper back to it which was impossible to remove. I was never too sure what the teacher did with the silver paper, but we were told it was for the black babies in Africa.

Once a year, a priest from the African foreign missions would call to the school. He would tell us about the plight of the black babies and the work he and his fellow priests were doing. There was great excitement all round then when he handed out a card depicting Rosary beads to each child. What he would ask us to do, was to go to each house and ask for a penny for the missions and for each penny received you would put a pin hole in one of the beads. There were fifty beads in total. We would go to every

Home Wasn't Built in a Day

house in the village and ask for a penny for the missions. When the card was full you would bring the four shillings and two pence back to school for the teacher to forward to the priest. The poor old black babies did well out of us all; apart from the school, every shop in the village had a money box for donations, with the inscription, 'Penny for the Black Babies'. We weren't very well-off, but strangely we drew some sort of comfort from the fact that there were people out there who were much worse-off than us.

In November 1960, we heard on the wireless that some Irish troops were missing while serving with the United Nations in the Congo. We prayed at school each day for the safe return of the soldiers. Then it was reported that nine soldiers had been killed by the Balubas, a primitive tribe in the jungle. They had been savagely killed with spears and axes. I listened to the wireless at home when the coffins of eight men were brought back to Ireland for burial. One man could not be found. At school it was said that the Balubas ate him. What type of people would eat a human being? Then the teacher told us that this tribe knew no better. We still could not understand it. I cried so bitterly all day. I kept saying, 'I hate the Balubas, I hate the Balubas.' One thing for sure was that I never wanted to become a soldier, if it meant being eaten by the Balubas.

My uncle Mikie's health continued to deteriorate throughout 1961. I knew very little of what was going on, except that he was spending an increasing amount of time in bed. Mikie was seriously ill, dying with cancer. After a very short final struggle, he died on Christmas Eve.

He was a young man, in his early forties. This was a huge turmoil for the family. My parents tried to keep Christmas as normal as possible, but how could they? Christmas Eve was strange. Christmas Day even stranger! We all went to the funeral on Christmas Day. Our biggest concern was to get home as quickly as possible to play with the few things Santa had brought us. As children we did not fully understand what was happening and the sadness which surrounded the whole family.

My mother mourned his passing greatly, saying that poor old Mikie had a 'heart of gold.' My father also felt the loss and comforted and consoled my mother in her time of grief. My mother always said that anybody who died during the twelve days of Christmas went straight to heaven. This very much consoled her with the loss of Mikie. She also said at the time, 'I know now what Padre Pio meant when he said 'Mikie would be fine and in safe hands; he knew that Mikie would be taken from us and brought to heaven where he would be at peace.'

My mother's faith had once again helped her and consoled her in a time of trouble. From that day forward, she always lit a little candle on Christmas Eve. This candle was in addition to the Christmas candle. We knew well that this little candle was for Mikie, and it became as traditional as the lighting of the Christmas candle itself.

My father continued to work away with the Board of Works but the job became increasingly insecure. Occasionally, he was laid off through lack of work at the site where he was employed. He used to drive engineers from site to site. My father looked more like the chief engineer than the jeep driver. He was always clean-shaven and well-dressed, with a collar and tie. I would love to see him using a new 'Max Smile' blade as it meant I could

Home Wasn't Built in a Day

have the wrapper from the blade. The wrapper had a sketch of a baldy man smiling and when you turned it up side down it was an unshaven man scowling. My father thought the work of an engineer was very professional and of high standing.

He often said to me, 'Pat, if you don't go on to become a priest, an engineer would be a good job.'

I hadn't a clue what an engineer was or did, but I knew what a priest was all about. When my father would come home from work at night I would dress up as a priest using an old flour bag as a vestment. I would use a chair as an altar and a packet of silver mints as Holy Communion. Then I would say what I thought was Mass muttering away in pretend Latin for the family. My father and mother were very proud. They thought that I was sure to go on and become a priest. They even invited some of the neighbours in to see me saying Mass.

They loved to hear, 'Ye have the makin's of a priest in the family there.' As far as my mother and father were concerned, this was the first step in my journey to becoming a man of the cloth.

SIX

During the sixties in Ireland, any form of artificial birth-control was frowned upon by the Catholic Church. Across the water, in England, condoms were permitted and freely available. With many people over and hither to England, condoms were smuggled in to this country. However, local man, Christy Mulligan, always carried a healthy supply of 'French Letters' as they were then known. Emigrants who were not influenced by the wrath of the preaching Fathers would bring them back to Christy on returning from England. I'm pretty sure that they sold them to Mulligan at their original price but he sold them on at a premium.

Christy Mulligan was the local buy-and-sell merchant, who operated out of his little house in the middle of the village. He was the unofficial pawnbroker of the village. The sale of condoms was absolutely necessary. Venereal disease or the 'Clapp' as it was known then, was rampant so 'French Letters' acted as prevention. 'French Letters' were mostly used by the single people to prevent pregnancy.

A single woman who became pregnant was completely frowned upon, and was often forced to emigrate to England. She would have her baby there, where nobody

Home Wasn't Built in a Day

knew her. Alternatively, the man who 'got her into trouble' would marry her and they would stay and face the music together. With the influence of the Catholic Church, lots of babies were conceived by married couples in December. Inevitably when the man of the house arrived home for Christmas, the woman fell pregnant. It is amazing the amount of men and women in Ireland today that have an August birthday.

Most of my father's family emigrated to London, except for his brother the priest, who spent many years in the African Missions and one sister who married an Irishman and stayed at home. My uncle Jim, the priest, worked with the Holy Ghost Fathers in war-torn Nigeria. He served with his great friend, Father Joe Whelan from Carey's Road in Limerick City. Father Whelan was later promoted to Bishop of Nigeria. While much of Ireland was in a state of poverty, these men gave of their valuable time and expertise to a nation that was much worse-off than ourselves. The stories we heard at school made us realise this, and we were all very proud of uncle Jim and all the good he was doing in Africa. None of my mother's family emigrated, apart from her brother, Mikie, who had only managed to stay a few months in London with my father back in 1958. In most cases, once one of a family made the break and went to England, the rest of the family followed suit.

We always noticed those that returned home from England were dressed far better than those at home. In fact, I always thought that the English way of dress was posher and better than the Irish way. Also English people drank coffee, something that we never did; in fact, we had never even seen what coffee looked like. We were a nation of tea drinkers and had pigs head for dinner. If the truth was to be known, these people probably kept their best clothes to show off when they came home to Ireland.

The ultimate sign in announcing that you had 'made it' across the water was when you came home for a holiday, well-dressed and with the wife carrying a poodle dog on a lead. The poodle was the designer dog, kind of an upper-class, royalty thing. Well, that's how it was perceived here. This peculiar-looking animal was manicured and washed nearly on a daily basis. Again, we were a nation who only kept terrier dogs, whose coats only ever saw a sup of water when some auld woman would drown them with a bucket from the water fountain. Many a day you'd see an old lady giving two dogs who were in the act of love, a shower to break them up from the eyes of innocent children.

My aunty Nancy came home every summer, always sporting a poodle. She would come and visit us with her husband, John. My mother would send me across to Casey's pub for two bottles of stout. John loved his stout and my mother always ensured that he had a couple when they visited. We often joked about the accents that the emigrants developed after a short time in England. It was often remarked, 'Will you listen to that English twang and all he did was to go over there to check the time!'

Christmas 1962 was much different from other Christmases. There was a huge strain and a different type of uncertainty in the air. My father started to miss a lot of time from work. Missing a lot of time meant a lot less money. He was ill, couldn't eat, and was losing weight. He and my mother were worried, but as always, Christmas came and went and both my parents endeavoured to

Home Wasn't Built in a Day

make it a happy time for us. Then, in late January, 1963, he arrived home early from work clutching his stomach, barely able to cross the road to our house. He complained of terrible stomach pain and felt completely worn out.

'I need a doctor,' he said.

'I think them fags have you killed,' said my mother. 'Each morning all you have is a cup of tae and a fag.'

'I'm able for nothing more, Bridgie.'

My mother had, what she felt was an explanation for the decline in his health. Some weeks previously, a racing pigeon had flown into our house and decided to stay. The weather was very rough, with snow for many weeks, so I guess the poor bird was cold and hungry. He was a tame and friendly bird and we christened him Joe Pigeon. He was the pet we never had when we were growing up. Each evening I could not wait to get home from school to see Joe. Then in the height of my father's illness my mother raged; 'Get that pigeon out of here! Since he arrived here we never had an hour's luck.'

We were all so disappointed, but Joe Pigeon had to go. It somehow seemed that if the pigeon was got rid of, my father's illness would go too.

Like everyone at the time, my parents were very superstitious. Nailed to our back door was an old horse shoe. It was deemed good luck to have one in the house. Like many people of their time, lots of signs and events had meanings. For instance, the banshee was known to everybody in Ireland. She was the woman of the dead. The tradition was that when she was heard, it meant that somebody was about to die. A headless man would come down from the skies, riding a coach with two black horses to pick up the spirit of the deceased. My mother told us that the banshee usually appeared near a river, stream or loch, where she washed the blood-stained clothing of the unfortunate whose death she had come to foretell.

The banshee guarded each Milesian Irish family; these were the families whose names started with an O' or Mac. We were not an O or a Mac except if you spell it in Irish. For the purpose of the Banshee I spelt my name in Irish. As the story goes, the Banshee would follow the descendants of her family to England, America, Australia, or to anywhere in the world; she would never leave her family. When she appeared shortly before a death, she would wail sadly in frustration and rage. Not only her family, but many others in the area would also hear her eerie cry. I remember one old lady saying that the night before her husband died, she had seen the 'headless coach' passing by her front door. It transpired many weeks later that the so-called headless coach that night was none other than Liam Sullivan, pushing an old wrought iron bed back the street to his mothers!

When in bed at night we would listen for the wailing of the banshee. If we heard her wail, we would be very frightened. The following morning after hearing her, our first task would always be to find out who had died during the night. It seldom transpired that a death had occurred in the locality, but it didn't stop us believing fervently in the existence of the banshee.

In Ireland, people constantly look for unusual signs that have an effect on human life. Superstition played a big part in our growing up and for many people carried on into adult life.

Home Wasn't Built in a Day

There was, and still are, many unusual occurrences which cause people to be superstitious: clocks chiming irregularly, or stopping for no apparent reason; roosters crowing at night, or bees swarming at doors or windows to accompany a soul in flight to heaven. Birds such as owls, robins or crows, perching at windowsills or housetops have often been seen as harbingers of bad news. As for magpies, they always spelt disaster. To see one was a sign of bad luck. If you saw one magpie you would always look for a second one. One was for sorrow, two was for joy. Any one of us at home would never dare to walk under a ladder as it was deemed that some sort of bad luck would befall you if you did. If we saw a meteorite or a falling star in the sky, we would immediately bless ourselves, as this meant that a soul was going to heaven from purgatory.

We were all very much aware of the paranormal and the significant role it played in our daily lives. One of the main fears that people had, was to be the victim of *pishogs*. We would hear of a chunk of butter being smeared on the gate of a house. It would have been put on the gate by someone working *pishogs*, wishing ill on that household. Only certain people had the power to work this type of witchcraft. Many a family was cursed and bewitched by *pishogs*.

Sometimes the act of pishogary did not bring evil, but turned out to be some type of magic performance. My uncle Tony Cronin travelled many miles to a dance in north Kerry with his friend, Seamus Ryan, and his brother, Paddy. The three boys had cycled twenty miles to the dance hall and on their way home in the middle of the night they were stopped by a little old lady at a remote cottage. She said that she had just roasted a chicken and

Paddy Cronin

offered them a bite to eat. She brought the chicken out of the oven and on to a plate. She then served three chicken legs to the boys. The boys became suspicious with the three legs and refused to eat the chicken. They swore that they'd starve rather than touch a chicken with three legs. Day was about to break so they got on their bikes and rode to the nearest village. When telling their story to an old man in the village, he told them that nobody would step inside the door of that house, as the lady there was constantly working *pishogs*.

With money scarce, we would be delighted to see a spider pitch on us. It meant money was on the way. Likewise, if your left hand palm was itchy, it also meant that money was not far off.

'My palm is itchy Mama,' I'd say.

'Which one?' she'd ask.

'My right one,' I'd say.

'Oh, that means someone is going to shake hands with you, 'tis the left one for money' she'd say.

If your nose was itchy, it meant that someone was talking about you. Another sign of bad luck was the breaking of a mirror. We had a mirror in the kitchen, which was laid on the table and supported against the wall. My father would use it for shaving and combing his hair. Accidentally, I disturbed it, and it fell to the floor smashing into many pieces. Everybody became concerned, not for the loss of the mirror, but for the impending seven years of bad luck. It took the whole family days, if not weeks, to get over the breaking of that mirror, and I often felt that any misery that befell our family was my fault, for breaking the mirror on that fateful day.

SEVEN

The spring of 1963 was one of the coldest encountered in years. The snow and frost lasted for many weeks, but somehow, having snow on the ground did not excite me as a child, as there was a gloom about the house with my father's health in sharp decline. He was visiting the doctor on a regular basis and was taking a huge amount of tablets. It was thought that he had a stomach ulcer, but he would have to go to hospital for tests to confirm this. On the 6th of February he was sent to the Limerick Regional Hospital by our local doctor. It was the day before my ninth birthday. At the time, I thought it was the day before my birthday, until later when I discovered that my birthday actually fell on the fifth. When he left, I sensed that all was not well and that the situation could be very serious.

My father kept on saying to my mother, 'I have no bloody ulcer, I think I'm finished.'

'You're not finished, Johnny,' she would say.

Before he left, we all sat round the table for a meal. We never usually had anything out of the ordinary, but on this occasion, we had what seemed to be a very substantial meal. Dada hardly ate a bite. He wasn't able and was obviously worried. He turned to me and asked what I wanted for my birthday.

'A battery operated torch,' I said, 'One that allows you to change the colour of the light.'

Frank Gazette, who ran a local cinema had a bicycle shop down the road from us, and it was there that I had spotted the multicoloured torch. He gave me the couple of shillings for the torch and I headed off straight away to buy it. I couldn't wait to get home and show off my new acquisition; it was certainly a distraction from all that was going on around me.

My aunt Katie took my father to hospital. Although he had parted from the family many times in the past, seeking greener pastures across the water, this time was different. Leaving under a huge cloud of uncertainty made this occasion more poignant. In hospital, it was decided, after many tests, that he would have to undergo an operation. The news was not at all good. He was diagnosed with cancer of the colon. My mother told us that our father's fate was now in the hands of Holy God and that all of us must pray very fervently for him. She cried for days, all the time lighting candles to our Blessed Lady. After the operation, we all went to the Limerick Regional Hospital to see him. It was strange seeing him in a hospital bed. He looked different. He had lost a lot of weight, but he still had that loving father's smile on his face.

'Come sit beside me,' he said. 'Look' he said, 'there's where they operated on me,' showing me the large scar on his stomach.

My two sisters, who were also at the bedside, took no notice whatsoever of the goings on. They were too young

Home Wasn't Built in a Day

to understand. I imagine that he was showing me his wound to reassure me that all the sickness was over as the operation had cured him. The scar was proof that the doctors had done their job. I went in beside him, cuddled into his back, and fell asleep. I loved him and all about him, I missed him and now we were together again. I woke up to him holding me and crying bitterly. I think he must have known that time was running out, and that the end was near. My father was a non-drinker and throughout his life he wore a pioneer pin, demonstrating his abstinence from alcohol. His own father, Paddy, our grandad, arrived at the hospital with a couple of bottles of Guinness. My grandfather was a master pint drinker. He was Mr. Guinness himself! Every day of his life he would go to the pub and have his fill of the black stuff.

'Drink that, he said to my father, 'there's goodness in it; it will help to build you up.'

He drank it, and was pleasantly surprised.

'Have a dozen of those ready when I come home, Bridgie,' my father said to my mother.

We all thought that my mother would pass out, hearing my father ordering Guinness. Surprisingly though, she reacted in a very positive way by agreeing to his request. Neither one of the two of them had any great admiration for the drink but in times like these, situations and goal posts change. I suppose, somewhere in her mind, she knew that she probably would never have to fulfil his request anyway.

A few years previous, the locality was in the national news with the claim that the Blessed Virgin Mary had appeared near the church in Pallaskenry, which was only about five miles from us. On Sunday, April 16th 1961, a young girl claimed that she had seen an apparition of the Virgin Mary. Ann Murphy was only nine years of age, so her credibility would always be questioned, but in Catholic Ireland such a claim was taken very seriously by the people.

The whole of Ireland seemed to descend on Pallas. Our auntie Katie took me, my mother and my two sisters there for what was expected to be a 3pm appearance of the apparition on the following Sunday, April 23rd. The child had said that the Virgin Mary would appear to her while performing the Stations of the Cross in the church. She also said that the Blessed Mother would talk to her at the fourteenth Station.

The church was full on the day, the village having become a Mecca for worshippers, believers, sceptics and lots of curious onlookers. There were photographers and press people everywhere. Invalids were brought into the church on stretchers and in wheel chairs. One man who was terminally ill with cancer, travelled all the way from America in search of a cure. Most people were on their knees, waiting for a miracle to happen. Then, little Ann Murphy began the Stations of the Cross. The whole church was in silence as the young girl went from one Station to the next. The priest would announce each station as the little child prayed. Then she came to the fourteenth Station.

The Priest announced 'The fourteenth Station, Jesus is laid in the tomb.'

Everyone watched the young girl, who appeared to be in a trance, and all our family prayed for uncle Mikie,

Home Wasn't Built in a Day

who was very ill at the time. She kneeled at the station for a long time with her head bowed, and she seemed to be talking to the Blessed Virgin. Eventually the child was taken away by her father who was protecting her from the crowd. Everyone wanted to touch the child, who continued to claim she was talking to her Mother in heaven.

One amazing fact to emerge from the apparitions was that the date of the first apparition, April 16th, was the anniversary of the death of St Bernadette of Lourdes. The significance of the date was not apparent at the time, although later its significance was acknowledged. It also gave a certain amount of credence and validity to events, and a little bit more pondering for the many sceptics. During one visitation, it was reported that Our Lady told Ann Murphy that she would be taken to heaven as a young girl. Again, not much notice was paid to this at the time, but it did indeed come to pass, as Ann died as a young girl of eighteen. Mary Ellen Speran, who lived in the village at the time, was a mentor to little Ann Murphy. Ms Speran, now in advancing years, spoke to me recently about Ann.

'There was definitely something special about Ann,' said Mary Ellen, 'She was full of Grace and I would say a Saint. We prayed a lot together during the apparitions and I have no doubt about it. Our Lady did appear to her.'

The Pallaskenry church, the altar and the stained glass window behind the altar had always been dedicated to the Blessed Virgin Mary, so it seemed only fitting that such a place should have been chosen for her to appear. Well, that's what the locals thought anyway. The tree beside the church, where the first reported apparition had occurred became a relic, with people queuing up to take a piece of the bark. John Quilty, a local man was forever on top of the tree peeling bark and passing it down to the many pilgrims. John probably saw his good deed, in supplying the sacred bark to the pilgrims as an act of faith in itself and, in doing so, probably saved a lot of people injuring themselves in the process. We eventually got a piece, which we brought home. This relic we kept in the glass case in the kitchen and we often blessed ourselves with it.

During one of our visits to our fathers hospital bedside, I decided to take the piece of bark from the glass case and place it on his stomach. I knew that his stomach was the sick part of him. He was so delighted that I had brought the bark and he was completely filled with emotion by my little act of faith. My mother was also touched by my reverent thought and I suppose, in hindsight, she definitely thought that someday I would be a man of the collar. Even though my father was so ill, he also consoled himself in the thought that someday I might be ordained to the priesthood, just like his brother, uncle Jim. He held the piece of bark against his stomach and then raised it to his forehead and blessed himself with it. I was sure he would now be cured of his ailment.

We visited him in hospital on a couple of more occasions as a family. There were lots more cuddles with many more tears. On one of those last visits, he told us of a surprise visitor he had. It was the local Fine Gael TD, (member of parliament) Denis Jones. He could not believe that a man from the party that he had no time for, would come and visit him. There and then, he vowed to change his stance on politics and said that in future he would vote for the man rather than the party that was behind him.

Home Wasn't Built in a Day

The end was now nearing for my father, so as children it was probably decided to protect us as much as possible from what was about to happen. My mother would travel with my aunt Katie to the hospital each night to comfort and reassure him that he would make a full recovery. His passing was a bit sudden in the end, as it was expected that he would lasted a few more weeks. On Saturday, March 9th. my father's brother, uncle Jim, the priest, was due to go to the hospital to tell him that his time was limited and to prepare to meet his Maker. Before he arrived at the hospital, my father had already passed away. He was only forty-six years old.

My auntie Katie called to our house at eight o'clock that morning to break the terrible news to us. She did not tell us what had happened but asked us to go to her house with her. I will never forget that terrible moment when she broke the sad news to us all. My mother went into a state of hysteria. She had lost her best friend and her one and only love. They grew up together, they struggled together, she nursed him, and as she often said 'never put to nor from him.' I cried so bitterly with the thought that my father was no longer with us.

I kept saying; 'My dada is not dead, It's not my dada.'

I was sure that it was some sort of mistake. The hospital had given my aunt incorrect information. But soon the realisation began to sink in. I had lost a father that I dearly loved; a father who introduced me to the art of fly fishing on the banks of the river Deel; a father who brought me to Kenneally's house on Friday nights where stories were told and the Rosary was said with the greatest of reverence; a father who brought me to orchards picking apples and around the country selling them to make a few bob. Regardless of the circumstances, Mary, Breda and I would always have our presents at Christmas. Happy memories now flooded back to me of travelling to Hector Grey's in Dublin to view my potential Christmas present of a slide projector. There would be no more Saturday mornings in Woolworth's in Limerick to buy the yellow plastic pipe and the stick of candy rock. No more smoking the pipe with his cigarette end. The man who gave all, tried his best, loved his wife and family, had lost the final battle. The emptiness that I felt was beyond belief.

We were protected from the funeral hype by my aunts. There was no mention of death or funerals. My mother was in a deep state of depression. She took to the bed. She was a broken woman with no future. Uncle Jim, the priest, came and spoke to us. He told us children that our father was now in heaven. He wanted to make sure that we fully understood it. My sister Mary was only five years old and Breda just four. They were far too young to understand what was going on.

My auntie Eileen went to my mother in her bedroom and said, 'Bridgie, you have three young children to live for and you owe it to them to keep going; Johnny would expect that.'

That shook my mother back into reality. It prompted her to begin a new phase of her life.

For many weeks and months I sat on the inside of our front window, crying and somehow expecting that my father would come home again, but he never did. I suppose being young and innocent I believed that he would come back as he did so many times in the past.

A few months after his passing we were listening to Radio Eireann on the wireless and I became inconsolable when *Goodbye Johnny Dear* was played.

Just twenty years ago today, I held my mother's hand,
As she kissed and blessed her only son, going to a foreign land;
The neighbours took me from her breast and told her I must go,
But I could hear my mother's words, tho' they were faint and low.

Goodbye, Johnny dear, when you're far away,
Don't forget your dear old mother far across the sea;
Write a letter now and then and send her all you can,
And don't forget where e'er you roam that you're an Irishman.

That song brought back so many memories for me. I honestly thought it was about my own father. From the moment of his death, and for many years to come my mother's black dress code was a constant reminder of our sad loss. This was not unusual at the time in Ireland as widows would generally dress in black after the loss of their loved one. Many of them, especially older ladies, who had lost their spouses would continue this dress code until they passed away themselves. In my own mother's case as she was a very young widow, the black clothes eventually changed to dark colours and in wasn't for many a long day that she chose to wear something a little more cheerful.

I often wondered what it would have been like to have my father into adulthood. The conversations we could have had about the many aspects of life, the guidance and direction he would have given me into my teenage years and beyond. To talk to him on a one to one, man to man would have been wonderful, but something that now sadly I would never be able to have.

EIGHT

Knock Shrine in County Mayo is probably the Holiest and most devout place in the whole of Ireland. Ireland is well noted for its devotion to the Blessed Virgin Mary, and it was there that an apparition of the Blessed Virgin, Saint Joseph and Saint John was reported in August,1879. It was no great surprise then, when my mother suggested that all the family should to go to the Holy Shrine to pray for our late father and to give us all strength to cope without him. It was late autumn, just seven months after his death when auntie Katie, who had a car, was to drive us. It was an early rise on a chilly October Saturday morning, when we were to set off on the 120 mile journey to Knock. As Katie started up the car and as we were getting into it, we noticed that the roads were very icy. Overnight there was a very heavy frost, which resulted in the roads being treacherous. Katie decided that it was too dangerous to venture on such a long journey, so we returned back home and decided to leave our pilgrimage for another day.

Instead of the planned Holy journey, I decided to play in our backyard with my two sisters. I made a swing from an old rotten rope, which I had found on the side of the street. I suspended the rope from a rafter on a shed. I tried to swing on the rope but unfortunately, it broke and I hit the ground, breaking my arm. Immediately, I ran into the house and told my mother that I was feeling sick. I don't know why I did not tell her that I had fallen. She put me to bed to sleep off the sickness, but when I woke up in a couple of hours I could see that my arm was very swollen and extremely painful, so I confessed to what had happened.

That evening, my mother organised for Katie to take me to the Limerick Regional Hospital. I was X-rayed and put in a plaster of paris as my arm was indeed broken. The plaster of paris was a great novelty. I was imagining all the admirers I would have when I got home and all the interesting things that every child from one end of the village to the other would write on it.

Katie then brought me into the city on my first visit to a supermarket. A new large shop, known as a supermarket had opened in O' Connell Street in Limerick. It was called the Five Star, and it was the talk of the town at the time. It was a peculiar place. It even had music playing in the background. You could go in there and pick out what you wanted and pay at the door on the way out. Strange, I thought! Anyhow, Katie bought me a packet of Maltesers. What lovely sweets! I had never seen or tasted anything like them before!

As a nine year old, I was frail and considered delicate. I developed a red rash on my forehead and I was told by my mother that it was ringworm. There was no need for a doctor to diagnose what it was; my mother knew exactly what ringworm looked like.

Paddy Cronin

An old lady who lived about two miles from us had a secret potion to cure the horrible rash. Her name was Mrs. Willy Harry Ruttle. I would travel to her house with her husband, Willy Harry, on his ass and trap. He would be on his way back from the creamery after delivering his milk. I swear to God, the journey in that ass and cart with Willie Harry was the sorest that anyone could ever make. Every hole, bump and cobble on the road vibrated up my backside.

Whenever I passed a Catholic church, I would traditionally make the sign of the Cross. On my journey with Willie Harry, we would pass the local church but I would never bless myself. He was a Protestant and I was shy to make the gesture in the presence of a non-Catholic. I suppose I was also fearful of somehow insulting him. At the time, I felt that I was committing a grievous sin, as at school we were taught to be open about our Faith. The Catechism decreed that we must 'Profess our Faith openly and pray earnestly for the Grace of God.' Oh well, I thought, just another sin to confess!

Whatever about my dreadful sin, I felt that I had enough penance done on that donkey and cart. I was glad that I always made the journey home by foot. It gave me a chance for my backside to chill out. As well as that, I would bless myself about ten times passing the church to make up for my sin of not blessing myself on my way there.

Saturday morning was my standing appointment with Mrs Ruttle, who would rub this revolting liquid on to the rash. Oh, 'twas so sore! I guess that half the country had ringworm, as she used to have lots of people coming and going to the house. I always kept it quiet that I had

Home Wasn't Built in a Day

ringworm. I thought it was only poor people who lived in bad conditions that got this red raw rash. It was very much a taboo subject and no-one ever discussed it.

I often asked Mrs. Ruttle, 'How long will it take for this thing to go away?'

All she would say was 'call again next Saturday.'

Eventually it cleared, but I was never sure if my cure was actually as a result of Mrs. Ruttle's magic potion.

The first Christmas after our father's death was always going to be a sad one. Most people throughout the country were trying to come to terms with the death of President John F. Kennedy. The John Kennedy tragedy had very little impact on us, as we could not see beyond our own father's death. Even the death of Pope John XXIII, which happened in that same year, barely touched us.

I decided to place a crib on our front window at home. I made the crib from a cardboard box and my sisters made figures of the Holy Family from plasticine, or *morla*, as we called it. My mother gave me a couple of shillings and I bought a flash lamp battery and small bulb at Frank Hanley's shop. I connected the tip of the bulb to the tip of the battery with silver paper that I got from a cigarette box and this lit up the bulb. I then put the light in the crib and placed it on the front window. We would go across to the other side of the road and see crib lighting. We were all so proud!

This particular Christmas was also my first time going to midnight Mass. What an amazing experience! There was wonderful singing by the choir, but also hilarious moaning, groaning and cheering from the few drunks who had made their way to the back of the church. Going to midnight

Paddy Cronin

Mass for the first time was a major step in growing up. My mother had now promoted me to man of the house. I liked the responsibility and I was also given the task of ensuring Santa called to my two young sisters.

Presents had arrived from our aunt Nancy in England, and my mother and I ensured that they were laid carefully at the foot of the bed. My mother was in deep mourning for my father and the emptiness that she was suffering was felt by all of us. If we were a family of profound faith, then we were now even more immersed in prayer. My mother lit many candles and had us all pray fervently for the souls of our father and uncle Mikie. However, like all other children, our first priority was Christmas and playing with our new toys.

In the early sixties a new pastime was fast developing, watching television. My father had been right; television was on its way and it would change all our lives forever. We did not have a TV, nor did any of our neighbours. Frank Ruttle, a local man who repaired bicycles, brought the first television to town and displayed it in his front window. Droves of people congregated outside his house each evening watching a very snowy RTE in black and white. RTE, was the new Irish national television station, called Radio Telefis Eireann, and everyone, everywhere, wanted to see what it had to offer. People came from neighbouring villages, not just from our parish, to view the new phenomenon. Word was well out that a television was on display in Askeaton.

'Jaysus! 'twill be the ruination of everything!' said Mickey Kenneally, as he watched with throngs of people, who were completely mesmerised.

Home Wasn't Built in a Day

'Oh, Holy God above in heaven, 'tis a new lease of life to us all!' said little Kitty Ruttle in her soft husky voice. Kitty had the nickname, 'Kitty The Hare.' She was named after the great spooky storyteller in the Christian Brothers' monthly magazine, *Our Boys*. All good Catholic boys were compelled to read *Our Boys*. With this new invention of television *Our Boys* and similar magazines were fast becoming a thing of the past.

'That television is better than any wireless.' said Kitty, 'The next thing they'll have is someone doin' the twist on the screen.'

'Well, the devil split 'em, whoever does that filth in front of dasent people,' said Christina Cronin, who was never a lady to mince her words. She made her way from the other side of the village to see what all the fuss was about.

The 'Twist' was a controversial subject at the time, as it was alleged that the devil himself had appeared in the Stella ballroom in Limerick in the 1950s, while some sort of dance involving provocative body movement was being performed. A lady had been asked to dance by a handsome young man and after they had been dancing provocatively he asked her to the mineral bar for a drink. Whatever look she gave, she noticed that he had cloven feet and she fainted. The man disappeared and afterwards it was deemed that he was the devil. Priests were called in to bless the hall the following morning and even a statue of Our Lady was erected in the ballroom to ensure a Holy presence in an unholy place. Our local priest, Father O'Dea had spoken from the altar on many occasions about the immorality of this new type of dance, which was becoming a worldwide craze. Partners did not touch while twisting, but in the eyes of the Church it was too suggestive.

'It portrays a sense of intent,' Father O'Dea would say.

I had no idea what he meant by this.

'Tis nearly as bad as a woman wearing a trousers, and by the way any woman wearing a trousers will not be allowed inside the door of this church,' said the very irate curate.

Priests frowned at the arrival of television in Ireland. They warned that it should only be used to watch the news and for important announcements by bishops and cardinals.

I was totally amazed at this new invention called television. How on earth could we see people on a screen without a projector? Crowds would make their way to Ruttle's, well before the programmes started at five-thirty in the evening, to get the best vantage point possible. Everyone was chattering like mad, excited at what was about to come on the TV, and discussing what they had seen the previous evening. There was complete silence though at six o'clock when a holy picture appeared on the screen and a bell tolled for the Angelus. It was like an apparition from Heaven itself! Old men lifted their hats and caps and every man woman and child blessed themselves and recited the Angelus prayer to themselves. At times, if someone started reciting the Angelus out loud, the whole crowd joined in.

Many of the crowd stayed to the very end of the day's programmes, which was usually about eleven at night. Once a week, a huge crowd would gather to watch 'The Virginian,' which was an American western. The two main characters in this show were household names in

Home Wasn't Built in a Day

our community. James Drury, who played the Virginian himself, and Doug Mc Clure, who played Trampas, his associate, had now become very real characters locally. There was also another show, Mr Ed, the talking horse. People would also come in droves to watch this strange phenomenon called Mr Ed. In fact some people were absolutely convinced that the horse truly had the ability to be able to talk. The final programme each day was usually a nun or a priest reciting a prayer or some type of holy reflection.

After this, Frank Ruttle would appear at the window to unplug the television. He was like the bearer of bad news. The show was over and everyone had to go home. It wasn't for at least another year or more that the crowds lessened. More TVs began to appear in town and people had begun to finally get over their initial amazement. Nothing would ever again have quite the same impact in our community as the introduction of television.

NINE

The Widow's Pension was £3 10s a week, a paltry sum for my mother to be able to make ends meet and to keep three young children. Our neighbours were good to us though, within their own financial capabilities. This was an era when most people had little but still shared a lot. Aggie up the road would keep my mother company, sometimes into the late hours of the night. Gretta Fitzgerald would bring jelly and trifle each Sunday, which we looked forward to immensely. Mrs Sheahan, who had a few cows, provided us with milk. The Mc Knights who lived across the road helped us in every way possible and Margaret Mc Knight's mother, Mrs Ruttle would often bring us an apple pie. Kathleen Daly, who was another neighbour, stayed with us at night for many months after our father's death, and another lady, Ann Purcell, whose father John was a relation of my mother, also stayed with us.

With the death of our father, we all felt a sense of loss and insecurity, so having someone stay with us helped us all greatly. My father's death brought a huge amount of stress on my mother. She was forever having headaches. She would often send me to Johnny Mulcair's shop for a Mrs Cullen's Powder. I was fairly sure that the powder

Home Wasn't Built in a Day

should have been dissolved in water, but my mother never did that. It was back with the head and straight down the hatch with the raw powder. She almost got instant headache relief from the Mrs Cullen's. It was well known as a cure for many an ailment and if this magic powder didn't shift it, it was usually time to see the doctor.

We would never turn the electric light on in the house until my mother deemed it to be absolutely necessary. Luckily enough, there was a street light right opposite our front door which gave us full vision in our front room when night would fall. That light would come on about six in the winter. Christina Cronin, an old lady who was a cousin of ours would call each evening on her way to Fitzgibbon's dairy for her pint of milk. She would wait in our dark front room until the street light came on. She knew then it was six, the time that the dairy opened.

As the street light would come on and light up our front room she would always make the sign of the Cross and say, 'Light of God to the Holy Souls in Heaven.'

I often said, 'Great, light for the poor souls here on earth as well!'

Michaelin Sheahan would also bring the odd cake to us as a little treat. This was usually a Swiss roll made by Gateaux Cakes. Michaelin was not the most well-off person in the world and I think that his gesture was mostly a spiritual one. Each Sunday night he would call to the house and take me to the Church devotions. Benediction and adoration of the Blessed Sacrament took place once a week and I was compelled to go. During the ceremony the church was filled with the sweet-smelling aroma of incense and the singing with great fervour of uplifting hymns such as *Sweet Sacrament Divine* and *I'll sing a hymn to Mary*.

I'll sing a hymn to Mary,
The Mother of my God,
The Virgin of all virgins,
Of David's royal blood.
O teach me, holy Mary,
A loving song to frame,
When wicked men blaspheme thee,
To love and bless thy name.

Once every month, 'Holy Hour' was held. This was a full hour of adoration and prayer on a Sunday night, even though we had already been to Mass on Sunday morning. My mother also ensured that we went to confession once a month. It was always the same rigmarole.

'Bless me Father for I have sinned.'

'How long is it since your last confession, my dear man?' The priest would ask.

'A month, Father,' I'd say.

'So, go on.'

'I cursed, Father. I gave back cheek to my mother, and I was shy about blessing myself when I passed the church.'

The priest usually gave three 'Our Fathers' and three 'Hail Marys' for penance. The best part of confession was waiting to see who was going into the confessional box and seeing how long they spent inside. If somebody spent any bit of time in there, we would all speculate as to the grievous sin they might have committed.

Willie Purcell who was known as 'The Merlo', one evening spent about an hour in the confessional. The speculation then started as to what crime 'The Merlo' had committed. Some said that his sin was so grievous that the priest took the hour to ponder what penance would suit his crime. About a week later Fr Mac Carthy met 'The Merlo' in one of the local shops and continued the conversation they had in the confessional box. This time everything was said out loud for all the customers to hear.

'God, Willie I really enjoyed our chat in the confessional about your exploits in the British Army, fighting for the Queen of England,' said Fr Mac Carthy.

'The Merlo', who was forever boasting about his service to the Queen and how he had a weekly pension from 'Her Royal Highness', could not resist telling his story to Fr Mac Carthy in the confessional box.

Confession consoled us greatly. Once you had confessed to the priest, the slate was clean, whether you were truly sorry or not, and for the most part, we were sorry for our misdemeanours. There were two types of confession – well, that's what the teachers told us at school. There was Confession of Contrition and Confession of Attrition. Confession of Contrition was when you confessed your sins to the priest and were sorry because you loved God, and as part of your sorrow you would sincerely vow to refrain from sin again. Then there was Confession of Attrition. This was when you said an act of Contrition to yourself because you were afraid of your life that you would die in a state of sin and burn in the fires of hell. The Confession of Attrition was obviously a much easier option, as then you would be spared the embarrassment of telling the priest face-to-face about your wrong-doings. However, we did not have much choice in the matter, as my mother was always the boss when it came to religious affairs, and insisted that going to church and making a 'proper confession' to a priest was the only true way to be sure of God's forgiveness.

As a present for collecting me each week for church, I would give Michaelin a bag of conkers. I would only give him small ones though. The larger ones I would keep for conker games at school. In early October, I'd pick them from chestnut trees. The conkers were inside a hard skin, like a small unripened apple. I would collect the conkers and put them on the front window at home to dry out and season. The longer I left them there, the harder and better they were. I would then pierce a hole through the conker and thread a one foot length of cord through it. At school we'd have a game where you would hit the other guy's conker with yours and try to break it. Many times we'd miss, leaving the other poor soul with sore fingers. The country boys at school had the best conkers. They had a lot more trees to choose from, so they could pick the finest and the biggest. John O'Brien had a conker that must have lasted the whole season.

Many a conker game ended up in fisticuffs. When a boys fingers were hit, sometimes he would think that it was deliberate and then the real fight began. All of us would then form a circle and the two would fight it out, usually until one of the bigger boys intervened, or worse still, if the teacher came upon it. Of bigger consequence was if Guard Kelly got to know about it. Every young fella was afraid to step out of line with Guard Kelly around. He never missed a thing! If he did, Guard Mac Gough, who was forever patrolling the streets on his bike, certainly didn't.

Home Wasn't Built in a Day

Now Michaelin Sheahan was probably in his seventies so what on earth was he doing with conkers?

'I sew them to my pants, boy.' he said, 'They keep away the piles.'

What on earth are piles I thought? Maybe it's some sort of a disease that old men get. Michaelin lived in a little house in the Lane. It was very cold and damp and not immune from the odd rat or two. I knew that, as he would ask me to walk him home from our house at night and he would never allow me first in the door of his house.

'Let me first in there' he would say, waving his walking stick and beating it across his bed. 'You can never be sure about them auld things comin' up from the river.'

On many occasions I saw a furry fella with a long tail run from his door. They frightened the livin' daylights out of me! Michaelin never seemed to mind too much though.

My father's sister, our aunty Nancy, continued to send us the usual parcel at Christmas. There was usually a little toy for each of us, but as we were getting older there were less toys. Most of the parcels now contained clothes. Clothes did not bother me and for the most part my trousers always seemed to have a patch on the behind. Simple wear and tear caused the backside to ravel but my aunts always did their best to repair the damage. They would sew a patch on using some of the inner lining so as to match up the colour. If there was insufficient lining, another piece of fabric was used which usually made the patch-up very conspicuous. Mind you, lots of young lads sported a patch on their trousers so it never seemed to bother me too much.

Paddy Cronin

I would go to the post office in the square each Friday to collect the widow's pension for my mother. One week I arrived home without the pension money, having lost it on the way. We searched the streets but to no avail. We often wondered about what happened to the money. It seemed unlikely that it was lost on the street. Despite most people being badly off, honesty always prevailed. If someone had found it, it would most likely have been handed up to the priest. Sometimes at Sunday Mass the priest would announce that money had been found and that it could be collected afterwards in the sacristy. Sunday after Sunday we waited, but no announcement. We came to the conclusion that the money which was all in notes had blown in over the bridge and was lost in the river.

Each Saturday afternoon my mother would have me watch out outside our front door for Mai Howard. She was the local relief officer who travelled from Pallaskenry to hand out vouchers to those who qualified as being disadvantaged. Once I spotted her walking past our door, my mother would have me go to the dispensary to collect our voucher. I wasn't the only one heading for the dispensary. Once Mai Howard got off the bus a steady stream of youngsters and older people alike formed a trail behind her all the way to the dispensary. I was never sure what the voucher was worth, but I think my mother would cash it in at the local post office.

As if it wasn't bad enough waiting for Mai Howard and the voucher, waiting for the farmers on their way home from the creamery was a lot worse. Every Saturday morning, the street would be lined with horses and carts and donkeys and carts, driven by the farmers on their way to the local

Home Wasn't Built in a Day

creamery with their tankards full with their week's milk. On their return, they would have skim milk from the creamery which they used to feed their calves. My mother would have me out on the street with a gallon tin. I would hold the gallon up to the approaching farmer in the hope that he would stop and give me a pint of the skim. When the gallon was almost full I would bring it back home.

My mother would use the milk to bake the finest bread in town. I loved the way her soda cakes were always finished off with the sign of the Cross. This was just a traditional way of dividing the bread, but at the time I thought that it was a holy gesture. Through time, I got to know the farmers who were generous and only those ones would I hold the gallon up to.

I would also gather milk for my aunty Eileen's pigs. She kept a few pigs and the skim milk was part of their diet. I was fascinated with pigs as we were told that they could see the wind. Not being the most outgoing young lad in the world, asking for the milk was always difficult. Sometimes, while nobody was looking at me I would go to the water fountain in the street and take a gallon of water and mix it in with the milk. This increased my volume, which meant I had less farmers to pester. There was one particular farmer that I was warned never to take milk from. I was told that he was working *pishogs*, and dairy products were associated with *pishogs*. Accepting milk from him would bring his *pishogs* into our house and that was something that we most definitely did not want.

John Nash, who lived up the road from us, had a terrier dog who was expecting pups. He promised me a pup once they were born and free to leave the mother. I counted the weeks and days to the pups being born. I did not tell my mother about the promise of the new pet. She would never have allowed me to have a dog. So the pups were born and one evening I arrived home with this young terrier, whom I had named Spot.

To my surprise, everyone liked the dog, including my mother. My first task was to have Spot's tail cut short. Johnny Sullivan was the man in the locality for cutting off dogs tails. I called to Johnny and with the flick of a pen-knife, off came the little puppies tail. It was cruel I suppose, but I was told by everyone and anyone that no terrier should have a long tail.

After a couple of months, I sensed that my mother wanted to get rid of the dog. With rabbits plentiful, I had a massive brainwave. Off I went with Spot to all the fields in the locality. Alas, the poor old dog had no interest in hunting rabbits.

On my way home through the local terrace houses Lena Mac Carthy called me, 'Hey little boy,' she said, 'where are you coming from?'

'I was hunting with Spot, I said.

'Did you kill anything?'

'No Ma'am,' I said.

'And what were you after?'

'A rabbit for the dinner,' said I.

The woman took compassion on me and asked me in.

'Michael was out this morning, she said, and killed four; take one home with you boy.'

Off I went down the street, as proud as punch with Spot by my side, proudly holding the rabbit. I met a few people on my way, all complimenting me on my hunting prowess.

'Well done young Cronin'

I brought the rabbit in and presented it to my mother. 'Where did you kill him?' said my mother.

'Down behind the school,' I answered. 'He's a great dog,' I said.

I was now convinced that my mother would let me keep the dog, as in her eyes he might have proved himself to be a useful hunter. I was wrong. One morning I got up and Spot was gone. My mother had given him away. I cried for days. She had no choice. She told me that he had a dose of the mange. I did not know what mange was but it sounded like a very nasty disease. She tried to console me by saying that Michaelin Sheahan had promised us a cat and that a cat was a far better option anyway as it would keep mice away from the back door. Sadly for me, a cat was a very poor replacement for Spot who had become a very dear pet and my best friend. After all, this was the first animal or pet that we ever had at home, and to suddenly be without him left me with a gaping hole.

Once again memories flooded back to me of a loved one lost; the death of my father, who was never to return, and now I felt that I was on my own once again, mourning for the loss of poor old Spot. No one really understood the intense sadness that I felt after Spot's departure, or the reasons why it affected me so much.

TEN

The reputation of schoolteacher, Gus O'Brien had preceded him for years. Every generation had their own story to tell about his toughness and no nonsense approach. I was just ten years old when I progressed to his class. I feared him being my teacher, not least for all the stories that had emerged from one year to the next.

He was a teacher of the 'old school' mentality, in that he was passionate about his teaching, and for him it was indeed a true vocation. God knows, and in hindsight everything he did was with the best will in the world. He would make us sing in class irrespective of whether we had a note in our head. The consequences of not satisfying his standards usually meant your hair being pulled, with most of us in class having had our hair cut short to avoid this.

John O'Brien was the tallest in the class, much taller than the teacher. We envied him as the only way he would feel the wrath of Mr. O'Brien's hair pulling was if he was sitting down. John ensured that he spent a lot of time standing by the wall. The one sure way to achieve this was to miss questions or not pay attention. Not alone did we envy John's tallness but also the fact that he was the only one of us in class that wore a long pants. Wearing a long pants meant that you could tear through the nettles and the briars without the burns and cuts. He told us that his father bought him the long pants in Burtons in Limerick. One afternoon after school, I asked my mother to buy me one in Burtons but her answer was a firm 'No.'

'God help us boy, be glad for what you have; that boy of the O'Brien's has a long pants because he is too tall for the short ones, and anyway I couldn't afford to go to Burtons. As well as that, his family are well off farmers.'

Singing in the class was at ten o'clock which usually began with *Beidh aonach amárach i gContae an Chldár*.

Beidh aonach amárach i gContae an Chldár
Beidh aonach amárach i gContae an Chldár
Beidh aonach amárach i gContae an Chldár
Cén mhaith dom é? Ní bheidh mé ann

'S a mháithrín, on ligfidh tú 'un aonaigh mé
A mháithrín, on ligfidh tú 'un aonaigh mé
A mháithrín, on ligfidh tú 'un aonaigh mé
A mhuinín ó, ná héiligh é

There were a few so-called crows in the class and they suffered because of it. I wasn't too bad a singer, but I was absolutely terrible at remembering the Irish words. I suffered the same consequences as the crows; the wrath of Mr. O'Brien and the inevitable wake-up call, which usually was a pinch on the back of my neck, was never far away. Later on, I admired what our teacher, Gus O'Brien, tried to achieve and the great appreciation of local history he managed to instil in us. He saw learning not just as a means to achieve academic excellence, but as the way we would learn to appreciate our culture and heritage. This was something we would not realise until much later on.

Friday morning we would sing the Nationalist songs. Friday was the day you had pride in your nation. All of us in the class cared little about nationalism, as our biggest fear was not remembering the words of the songs or the many questions that would be fired at us after the singing was over.

'Who was Sean South, Healy?' Mr. O'Brien would ask.

'He was from Garryowen, sir.'

'Who was he though?'

'He wrote a song, sir.'

'What? He didn't write a song Healy.'

'A song was written about him.'

'Stand out by the blackboard, Healy.'

'Sean South was an Irish Nationalist who led a group of volunteers to the north of our country on New Years Eve, 1956 and died for the cause; any fool would know that.'

And then he'd say, 'And who are the Beatles, Healy?'

'The greatest band in the world, sir.'

Mr. O'Brien would put his two hands over his face and turn into the corner of the room in a state of deep depression. The whole place would be in silence. After about two minutes he would emerge from the corner and take the familiar long strides up and down the room, pulling sternly on his braces with his head and face pointed towards the ceiling. We knew he was angry. You could hear a pin drop. The predictable litany of words from him which we must have heard hundreds of time throughout the year reverberated throughout the room.

'Oh Holy God, why do I bother?'

Home Wasn't Built in a Day

'This job is not a vocation, but a cross given to me by the Lord himself; romantic Ireland's dead and gone, it's with O'Leary in the grave!' 'Tis all bloody Beatles, 'Rollin Bloody Stones' but no bit of culture.'

After the outburst, calmness would descend upon the class once more and the singing would resume again. Mr O'Brien would hit the tuning fork on the desk and would sing aloud; 'Do re mi fa so la ti do. Now everyone, Do re mi fa so la ti do'

We did them bloody scales for what seemed like hours and hours, and when Mr O'Brien thought we were in sufficiently good voice, he would say with great pride, 'So now boys, show us your little bit of culture.'

Then everyone would sing his favourite song;

It was on a dreary New Year's Eve, as shades of night came down
A lorry load of Volunteers approached a border town
There were men from Dublin and from Cork, Fermanagh and Tyrone
And the leader was a Limerick man, Sean South from Garryowen

Mr O'Brien would march up and down the room checking everyone's vocal ability. I usually got the inevitable twist of the ear as he said, 'Come on, Cronin, you're pretending to sing.'

In truth, I was terrified by the whole atmosphere and felt intimidated by the entire school thing. I wasn't a bad student and did reasonably well at my books, but I found it hard to concentrate, because my mind was often elsewhere, mostly thinking about Spot and what he might have been getting up to. Mr. O'Brien would sometimes notice that I was not as attentive as I should be and would say, 'Come on, Cronin, you're away with the fairies.'

When it came to our singing lessons I was pretty good, so I did not have to endure Mr O'Brien's wrath too often.

Frequently on Sunday evenings, a relation of my mother, John Purcell, would bring me to his house in Limerick to sing. I wasn't the only one there to perform though. Anyone who had a note in their head was invited to John's house on Sundays. That was the same John whose daughter Ann had stayed with us after my father's death. John had bought a tape recorder which was a very unique item at the time. He must have recorded hundreds of people singing. To actually be able to hear your own singing voice being replayed, was something very special.

John was an ambulance driver for the Limerick Regional Hospital. Only once did I see John in his job as an ambulance driver, when he called to our house when I was very young, probably about three. He was collecting Babe Ann Sheahan to take her to the County home in Newcastle West, which was known as 'The Home o' Newcastle.'

Babe Ann was old and feeble and literally on her last legs, and was being moved to the home to die. By God, did she smoke! Like a trooper she did, with a Woodbine cigarette forever in her mouth. She was a cousin of my father's and she stayed with us for a few years. I think she originally had the key to the door of our house and invited my parents to take over the tenancy provided she had a room until she died. For many years, she and her sister Nora had a butcher's shop there. In fact, an old shed in our back yard was known as the 'slaughter house.' Although no animal had been slaughtered there for years, it still had the smell of decaying carcasses and congealed blood. 'Twas well said that, as a butcher, Babe Ann would have a fag with an ash on it, the length of the fag itself, while she would cut and cleaver the meat. She had a throat which was hung like a turkey. It was frightening looking, but thankfully, it did not match her gentle character. My father told me that she had a goitre, whatever the hell that was!

John Purcell took immense pleasure in bringing his friends and work colleagues to his house and replaying songs that he had recorded on his tape recorder. My favourite song to sing for him was *Doe, a Deer*.

'Quiet everyone,' he'd say as he held his hand up.

Then he would drop his hand sharply and I would start.

Doe, a deer, a female deer
Ray, a drop of golden sun
Me, a name I call myself
Far, a long long way to run
Sew, a needle pulling thread
La, a note to follow sew
Tea, a drink with jam and bread
That will bring us back to do...oh oh oh'

I felt like a celebrity listening to myself on tape. It was like hearing myself sing on the wireless. My singing was now becoming somewhat of an embarrassment, as I would often go to a friend or relation's house with my mother and the first thing I would be asked was to sing *Doe a Deer*. What was happening was that John Purcell was taking his tape recorder to every conceivable person he knew and playing the recordings for them. So now everyone knew about my singing prowess; me though, I had begun to despise that stupid song.

In the summertime we would often go barefoot to school. We considered it a great novelty, but in truth it saved my mother from finding the money for the next pair of shoes.

Once a week, Guard Kelly would call to the school and address the class. We were all shivering in our boots – well, for those that had boots!

'Two bikes had the wind let out of their tyres last Sunday night outside Casey's pub, said Guard Kelly, I'm sure one of you knows all about it.'

You could hear a pin drop. Guard Kelly would straighten himself and fold his arms tightly and talk even louder 'Am I getting through to you? One of you knows the story.'

We were all frightened, even though we all seemed innocent. Then, after a long speech about respecting people's property and vowing to apprehend the culprits, Guard Kelly would leave. He never used the tactics my mother had at home. She was a master at getting the truth out of us.

'Open your mouth and stick out your tongue,' she would say. 'Tell the truth and shame the devil.'

If she suspected that we were telling a lie she would say 'Ah, there's a big black mark on your tongue.'

A black mark meant that we were telling a lie. We would take her at her word and confess to the lie. Knowing that we had committed a lie, sometimes we would refuse to stick out our tongue. We'd often run straight to the nearest shiny object, like the cover of a sweet gallon, and stick our tongue out to see if it had a black mark on it. The image from the cover was not always very clear, which

Home Wasn't Built in a Day

would always leave us in some doubt about my mother's conclusion that we were telling lies. If we had a mirror in the house, it would be much clearer, but since I had broken the only one we had, my mother was slow to replace it in case it was broken again and brought us further bad luck.

Far worse than school, was the visit to the dentist at least twice a year. This was the school dentist and we were all compelled to go. 'The butcher' as we called him, was located across the road from the school in the local dispensary. When your name was called in the classroom to go over, you had no choice. I swear, to pull a tooth he would put the pliers in your mouth and his knee against your chest and then give one almighty pull. Luckily enough we had an anaesthetic to freeze our mouths, although it never seemed enough to dull the pain sufficiently. Receiving the anaesthetic was horrid too, feeling every inch of that needle boring into your gum. Worse still if you had to have a filling, it was drilling and filling all the way and no anaesthetic even if you really needed one. Signs beyond, many of us much preferred to have the extractions and were left gummy and toothless as a result.

In the local streets we often played barefoot. In summer, hardly anyone wore shoes at all, but it was a disadvantage without shoes playing ball on rough footpaths or cobbled streets. Sometimes we'd play hopscotch, a unique game in that boys and girls could play it together. As part of the game we would mark eight squares on the footpath with chalk. We were never short of chalk. This was easy to come by at school, while the teacher's back was turned.

My favourite pastime though was trapping little birds. I would get an old cardboard box and put it in our back yard, propped up with a little stick. I would tie a piece of thread to the stick and bring it inside the back window of the house. I had a few crumbs of bread under the propped-up box. I'd wait for hours for a bird to go in for the bread and when he would, I'd pull the thread and the box would drop down, trapping the bird underneath. My biggest problem then, was catching hold of the bird, and when I did, I would keep it in an old tea chest for weeks. Eventually the little bird would die, or if it was lucky, my mother would insist on me setting it free.

The only bird that I would not dare keep was a robin. The robin was sacred. My mother told me that the reason they had the red breast was that when Our Lord was dying on the Cross, a little robin perched on the Cross and a drop of blood fell on him. All robins thereafter, carried that red spot on their breasts.

I had little luck with keeping wild animals anyway. I caught loads of little small fish known as minnows or collies, in the stream near the old mill. I kept them in a jam jar, but none of them ever survived beyond a week or two.

Liam Ruttle who lived across the road from us, told me to put a horses hair in a bucket of water and that eventually it would turn into an eel. He gave me the horses hair but again I had no luck. I watched that bucket every day and I eventually gave up. He was obviously knocking great fun out of my innocence, as day after day he would ask me if there was any sign of the eel yet.

Mind you, it was also said that if you put a horses hair on the palm of your hand when you were about to be slapped by the school teacher, the cane would split in two. I assure you that to my detriment, I failed miserably

Home Wasn't Built in a Day

here as well. Not alone did the cane not break, but my teacher at the time thought that I was into some sort of pishogary and doubled the amount of punishment. Liam Ruttle himself was well known as a fine horseman but also as a wonderful showman. He certainly made a show of me anyway! He was the first person I'd ever seen riding a bicycle backwards. He played to the gallery and always received applause for his showmanship.

Meanwhile, I was increasingly insecure having lost my father, and then Spot my dog. Being insecure certainly made me shy and nervous. I also suffered a lot on my way home from school in the evenings. One particular bloke would push and shove me and often give me a right old hiding. I never knew the reason why. I suppose I was skinny and appeared vulnerable, so I had little fight in me. At one stage, much as I dreaded school, I dreaded coming home even more. Eventually, I told my mother what was happening and she appointed one of the boys in my class, Bobby Horgan, to look after me. Bobby was my Guardian Angel and she never forgot it. On occasions, when she could afford it, she would give him a six penny bit. Bobby would keep the six pence until Saturday and would often use it to buy a bag of Dave Shanahan's chips. Dave's chips were an institution. It was the only place in town serving chips. You would have to go to Limerick city itself to get a bag of chips if it wasn't for Dave Shanahan. My mother frequently reminded me that Bobby was keeping a watchful eye on me at school, and that I would be safe under his wing. This was great consolation to her and even more of a relief for me.

ELEVEN

If medals were awarded for dignity, my mother would have been on the podium to receive the gold. She was a very strong woman, both mentally and physically. Mentally she was very determined and straightforward in her thinking and physically she took on huge tasks, more than any woman was ever expected to. Each evening after school had finished, she would take all of us to a place called 'The Island' about two miles from home, located on the banks of the river. There, we would gather firewood and stack it into an old pram. At the time, lots of people would gather little sticks or '*cipíns*' as they were known. They were great to start a fire with. This was a dangerous exercise though, as the fields were full of cattle and on more than one occasion we had to scamper for our lives.

We would walk the wood for ages. I had a mission of my own though, looking for fairies and leprechauns. In the wood we would see lots of what were called fairy mushrooms and I was convinced that the fairies and leprechauns owned them. I had this image of leprechauns sitting on giant mushrooms, mending shoes, as we had been told that they were wonderful cobblers. The prospect

Home Wasn't Built in a Day

of seeing a real live leprechaun brought me back to that wood every evening, although my mother told me that they would never let themselves be seen. I always lived in the hope that somehow she might have been wrong. It was well said at school, that a man from nearby Ballysteen had captured one and had him in a bag for weeks. I also thought that if we met a fairy, we would be granted three wishes, and after all it was every child's dream to be able to make a wish.

One particular evening I decided to go to a nearby derelict site, which had trees growing on it. I wanted to surprise my mother and filled a bag of sticks. It took me ages to break the sticks from the tree. I arrived home delighted with my bag full of wood and immediately my mother screamed, 'Take that wood out of the house, 'twill bring a curse down on top of us.'

'Why?' said I.

'That's elder,' said my mother. 'When they crucified our Lord, they beat him with elder.'

I learned there and then, that elder was never again to be brought into the house.

We often picked flowers and brought them home to my mother. Mother's Day was usually in March and we would take to the fields and pick daffodils for her. I also managed to learn the hard way about flowers and May Eve. On one particular May Eve, April 30th, I decided to pick flowers on my way home from school. Again, I met with the wrath of my mother, when I was promptly told to dispose of the flowers and warned never again to touch a flower on May Eve. It was deemed very unlucky to have anything to do with flowers on that day. Flowers were to be left for the

Paddy Cronin

fairies on May Eve. We were told that the fairies were in the best of humour on May Eve, with the music of their pipes heard all through the night, while they danced upon their 'rath' or fairy fort. Apart from the fairies, May Eve was very much associated with evil and bad luck, so before we went to bed on that night, my mother would shake holy water in every room of the house to ward off any evil spirits.

In the summertime, my mother would bring us to a place known as 'The Lep' which was the local swimming pool. This was a large pond on the river Deel. About twenty yards above the pond was a group of pot-holes which had fresh water flowing through them. Each Saturday evening she would wash us there. It made a refreshing change from the tin bath at home; nevertheless, it carried its own drawback, as we hated being washed in front of all the people who were swimming. As well as that, the water always seemed to be freezing, no matter how warm the weather was. No one took any notice though. There were loads of other children also being washed and I'm sure they were just as embarrassed as we were. She'd wash our hair and every part of us with a large bar of carbolic soap, and by God, were your eyes sore if it ever got into them! You'd be heard roaring for miles.

During this period I was plagued with sore, festering eyes. My mother claimed that it was from handling too many cats. After Spot's sudden departure, my mother had acquired a few kittens from Michaelin Sheahan, which over the space of the year had multiplied into at least half-a-dozen.

My mother said I had to go up to Doctor Fitzgibbon at the dispensary to see about my eyes. I hated going there as

Home Wasn't Built in a Day

the place was dark and always full of old men and women lined up along an old bench. Lots of them had lemonade bottles which were full. I discovered later that the bottles were not full with lemonade, but with pee. Everyone there had some sort of infection, so the doctor would tell them to bring a sample.

When my mother brought me to see the doctor, he said that I was very run down. He told her that I should be on a tonic called radiomulsion and that putting a hot bread poultice on the eyes should help them. I hated that bloody tonic. I was made to take two spoonfuls a day of the most vile tasting syrup. All it did was to make me sick and I'm pretty sure it did not help my eyes one bit.

Bill Sullivan went to the dispensary when he had the 'flu, and the whole place could hear his mother explaining to the doctor what had happened to him. His mother tried to be posh when talking, and while telling the doctor of Bill's ailment, she referred to a few dances that he had attended as 'balls'.

'So, what's wrong with this young man?' said Doctor Fitzgibbon,

'Well, doctor' she said, 'he has caught his death from gallivanting through the country.'

'Go on, go on . . .' said the doctor.

'Well doctor, he went to a ball in Cappagh and then to a ball in Rathkeale, and between the two balls he has caught an infection . . .'

I dreaded getting the sore eyes, as it meant my mother putting a hot bread poultice on them about three times a day to try and clear the infection. I hated this treatment, but if Doctor Fitzgibbon recommended it, I had no choice.

Paddy Cronin

It was so painful, much more than the fester itself. It was a strange cure I thought, but not as strange as the cure for a cut. As children, we often fell while playing. In fact, it was very much the norm to see almost every kid with gashed knees and elbows.

We used to play bowley with old bike wheels, and would search old dumps for broken bikes. We would remove the wheels, and then we would take off the tube and the tyre. The inner wheel with the spokes was the bowley. We would beat the bowley in front of us with a stick and race our opponent who would have another bowley. For sure, one or other of us would fall, resulting in the inevitable cuts and bruises.

This game was always played on the largest hill in the locality, which was a great place to build up the momentum and to travel fast. It was here that we also raced one another in soap cars that we made from old orange boxes and pram wheels. We would scour the locality for old prams and remove the wheels. The wheels were then attached to the box. Every young lad had a soap box car. Often six or eight of us together would race down the hill in our soap boxes. The very steep incline was known as the Lugs Hill.

On the hill lived a small little man known as Jim the Lug. He would sit and watch us all day. When a fall or tumble occurred, which was very often, he would always render his advice.

'Show me the cut,' he would say.

'Ok, boy, piss on it and 'twill be fine before your married.'

'Piss on it, Jim?' I'd say.

'Yeh boy, 'twill keep away the fester.'

Home Wasn't Built in a Day

By God 'twas sore to pee on a cut but, it seemed to work. There were always lots of casualties. It was worth it though, because we all wanted to be the soap box and bowley champion, as both titles were extremely prestigious and carried with them the admiration of every young lad of the village. My mother was never too worried about me playing in the soap box as she was well used to the cut knees and torn trousers. She was, however, totally averse to me owning or playing with a catapult. It didn't stop me having one though. I'd go and find a nice fork of a tree and cut it to size. Then, I'd attach a strong rubber band to it and the tongue of an old boot to hold the ammunition. We'd fire small pebbles from the catapults. As youngsters, we all had catapults, with our main targets being crows. Yes, catapults were dangerous, but thankfully, as luck would have it, somehow we all managed to escape serious injury.

We all thought that 'The Lug' Mac Mahon was a strange man. He chewed 'Clunes' plug tobacco all day and would spit a lot from chewing it. You would need to keep well back from him when in his company, as a large brown lump of scum could arrive your way. He had little direction, absolutely no discretion and even less mercy during emission. 'The Lug' was a fisherman who earned his living netting the river Shannon. He used to tell me stories of days gone by and especially about his father's funeral. He was out fishing on the river when his father died. Jim got stranded for two days as his boat ran aground on an island on the river. On returning home he found his father sitting on the chair, as stiff as a poker.

'The wake will be tomorrow night,' Jim announced to the townsfolk.

Paddy Cronin

And what a wake it was! The finest of whiskey and porter was ordered to the house to wake the old man. Before the wake though, the corpse had to be gowned and laid on the bed, but there was a problem. Having died on the chair, his father had stiffened up in a sitting position. Jim solved the problem by putting him into bed, stretching him out and tying him down with a rope. It seemed to work and the wake began. Many old stock and drinking pals arrived for the wake and one hell of a hooley began.

'Jaysus, we sang from dawn to dusk,' the Lug said to me.

During the singing, dancing and the telling of stories somebody cut the rope that was keeping the corpse down, and low and behold, he rose from the bed. People ran from the house screaming and more just collapsed onto the floor laughing. The Lug' was not taken in by any of it, as he reapplied the rope and coffined his father for the funeral.

'I would never fear the dead' said Jim, 'tis the living you have to beware of, boy!'

And how right he was!

TWELVE

I was nine years old and I had to rise early each morning as I was an altar boy and served Mass each day. The parish curate had come to the school to choose a few of us to serve at the altar and it was considered to be a huge honour to be one of the chosen few.

'I think you'll serve us well, Patrick,' Father O'Dea said to me. 'I want you in the sacristy this evening at four o'clock.'

The rest of the class were wondering why I was picked. My mother said it was a great privilege to have been chosen and that I was picked because religion was in the family, because my uncle was a priest. Serving Mass was high profile. It meant you had to learn Latin – well, sufficiently to be able to answer the priest in Latin, anyway. To be honest, us altar boys did not really have a clue about Latin. We were coached by the priest on how to answer his prayers. It was nevertheless a great honour to serve Mass and often in the street somebody would say to you, 'Aren't you an altar boy?' Being able to reel off the Latin gave me a great sense of pride.

The priest would recite, *'Dominus vobiscum.'*

I would reply with an intellectual tone in my voice as if I understood every word, *'Et cum spiritu tuo.'*

Paddy Cronin

I would stay awake in bed at night practising my Latin answers. My head was often a complete fuzz with . . .

'*Ad Deum qui laetificat juventutem meam,*'

'*Kyrie eleison, Christe eleison.*'

There were eight of us regularly serving Mass at the time. About four altar boys would arrive to serve each Mass on Sundays. I would always try to arrive first, as it was first come first served for duties at the altar. Holding the paten for the priest at Communion was always the best job with the highest profile. Better still, when a strange priest or a local priest who was posted abroad, returned to say Mass, he would always give you a half-a-crown. If we knew that there was a strange priest in town, we would always keep it to ourselves, in the hope that we would be the lucky recipient of a few bob.

Roach Kenneally who was a small bald man would always be in the sacristy for Mass. He would never go to Mass in the main church, because he was shy about his baldness; in the sacristy nobody would see him. The priests of the parish allowed him that privilege. He was good-humoured and always saw the funny side of life.

'Roach' was his nickname; I think his real name was Paddy. Lots of people in the community had nicknames. Some were very funny, since lots of people were nicknamed after different breeds of bird. There was 'Mickey The Goose,' 'Jimmy The Snipe,' 'Mick The Robin' and 'Jim The Hen.' Others were called after four-legged animals. Michael Ryan was known as 'Mike the Puck.' Then you had Mick Harte, who was affectionately known as 'Mick the Pig' as after a bellyful of whiskey he would make crude faces, unknown to himself, which resembled the snout of a pig.

Home Wasn't Built in a Day

People were given nicknames as a means of identifying them from other families with the same name. These nicknames were most often considered to be affectionate or endearing. Very often, if someone had a nickname, their real name was almost completely forgotten, so much so, that unless you referred to them by their nickname, people wouldn't know who you were talking about.

Roach, like most villagers, led a simple life and his home was really no different to most that existed in rural Ireland at that time. There was little or no access to toilets or running water and making several trips a day to the nearest fountain was the only source of water. Sometimes you even had to queue to fill up your buckets, as there was always someone in front of you at the fountain.

One commodity that proved useful to Roach and to many people was the sweet gallon containers that my mother had from time to time. She sold bulls-eye sweets and clove rock in the shop, and the sweets came in gallon containers, which were known as sweet gallons. People were forever asking my mother to keep them a sweet gallon, as some families would actually use it as a toilet in the absence of a chamber pot. Farmer's wives would use it as a container for brewed tea that they would send out to the meadows to the servant boys who would be saving the hay. My mother would be forever writing down the names of people that had booked the sweet gallons.

Mind you, the sweet gallon was not the only so called 'cast off' that was put to good use. Improvisation was the name of the game if you were not flush with money. For example, there was no such thing as a playpen to put young children in, or if there was, it was unheard of in our village. Many mothers used an empty tea chest to contain young children. My mother said that the three of us were reared in a tea chest! The empty tea chests were supplied by Kennedy's grocery shop down the road, but as popular as they were, they did not come close to the demand my mother had for the sweet gallon containers.

When nature called, Roach Kenneally would carry his sweet gallon into the bedroom and the hollow noise of peeing into it would echo round his house. He would then shout to his mother, 'Ma, do you hear the Angelus?' The sound, he thought, was mimicking the Angelus bell.

Roach was always good for a song in the pub. He was also a master of recitation. He could recite by heart the opening chapter of *Robinson Crusoe*. He would call for silence in the pub and with pride he would deliver: 'I was born in the year 1632, in the city of York, of a good family, tho' not of that country, my father being a foreigner of Bremen, who settled first at Hull . . .'

Roach would then bring the house down with his rendition of a very old song about nearby Croagh:

In Croagh I was born, and in Croagh I hope to die,
Croagh is the most misfortunate place that ever hired a boy.
For hiring with those farmers you never know your task,
'Twould be better to drown in the Falls of Donass.

Some years later, Roach eventually died, and being one of the 'old stock' there was a large turn-out for his funeral. Roach was the last of the boys in his family. As they lowered his coffin into the grave, his sister Agnes leaned over and shouted in 'Roach, tell the boys we were asking for them.'

Home Wasn't Built in a Day

She was hoping that Roach would pass on her regards to her late brothers. Ah well, that's faith, I guess!

Three times a year I would cringe at Mass with the anticipation of what was to come. This was the time when everyone's monetary contributions to the church were exposed. Those dreaded dues! Christmas, Easter and summer it was expected that you gave money towards the church and its upkeep. No matter how badly off you were, it was considered your duty to contribute. The priest would forewarn the congregation at Mass that the announcement was imminent.

'This Friday is the last day for accepting the dues, so I will be announcing your contributions at all the Masses next Sunday.'

When the time arrived, I was always petrified until I heard my mothers name being announced. No matter what your circumstances were, you had no choice but to contribute. Then would come the dreaded announcements. There was a cold silence throughout the congregation. Tom Lynch, Moig £3, Paddy 'Mart' Sheehan, The Quay £4, Michaelin Sheahan, Bury Lane 15 shillings, Bridget Cronin, Main Street 10 shillings.

Thank God, I'd say to myself, that that bit was over. It used to make me very uncomfortable, especially if I was on the altar serving Mass. After Mass, the inquiry would begin, who paid what, and who didn't pay. Discussions and whisperings often went on for days, so it was best to try and contribute some bit to avoid embarrassment.

The death of a certain Myra Donovan created a lot of confusion in the parish. I had been given a note by Myra's brother, Tom, to bring to the priest, which was the announcement of her death. I gave the note to Father O'Dea but he refused to read it out at Mass.

'Is that a joke?' said Father O'Dea.

'Tom Donovan gave it to me, Father,' I said.

'Well' said the priest 'she was dead as well a week ago and was still alive yesterday.'

The problem was, that as Myra was nearing death, her brother Tom decided he would send a telegram to the nephews in Dublin. Tom maintained that it would take at least two days for the telegram to reach Dublin, so he proclaimed that Myra had died in anticipation of her death in a couple of days time. The relations in Dublin immediately contacted the priest about the funeral arrangements. They requested Father O'Dea to organise the funeral.

'We don't want to overstress Tom as he has enough on his plate,' they said.

The priest contacted the local undertaker, John Mac Knight and read out details of the arrangements at Mass. He announced that her remains would be removed from her house at 8pm, on Monday evening. John Mac Knight arrived at the house early on Monday morning with the coffin and was met at the front door by Tom.

'I want to leave her in the bed that she died in, 'til it's time to remove her to the church,' said Tom.

This was in anticipation that Myra would be dead by the evening.

'You can leave the coffin in the front room,' he said to John Mac Knight, the undertaker.

People began to arrive at the house to pay their respects, only to find Myra still alive and sitting up in bed. One of the first people at the house to give her condolences was Lizzy Brandon from the Quay. Lizzy was sure she had witnessed a miracle. She saw the coffin was empty and that Myra was still alive in the bed. As people came in to pay their respects, they were met by Lizzy at the door, waving her hands and shouting, 'A miracle, a miracle, she has risen from the dead!'

Tom had some problem explaining the situation to the mourners, as Myra still hadn't died. He decided that the best course of action was to take flight to the fields behind the house. The nephews from Dublin arrived at the house and witnessed all the commotion. They found Tom out the back and he explained what had happened. They decided that it was best for all if they returned to Dublin and waited for the real call. After this, Myra Donovan was always referred to as 'The Resurrection Donovan.' The note that I had given to Father O'Dea was, in fact, correct, as on this occasion, one week after the original announcement, Myra had finally passed away. The priest did not read it out at Mass though, until he went to the Donovan house to see the dead woman for himself.

I was in Donovan's house only once in my life and it was an experience. I was there with my father when he bought his orchard of apples. Tom Donovan gave a new meaning to wall-papering. He had every room in the house wall-papered with sheets of newspaper from the *Irish Press*. Amidst all the newspapers, and in pride of place over the mantlepiece, was a picture of 'O'Donovan Rossa.' Tom claimed to be a direct descendent of the great Irish Fenian, and was very proud of the portrait adorning his mantlepiece.

Paddy Cronin

At the end of Sunday Mass, the priest would always say a prayer for the conversion of Russia. Russia was a communist country and it was seen as our responsibility for the salvation of their souls. Communists seemingly were bad people. Prayers for their conversion emanated from the reported apparitions of Our Lady at Fatima in Portugal in May 1917 to three young children.

During one of the apparitions, Our Lady revealed visions of Hell with all its fire and demons to one of the children. The thoughts of burning in the fires of hell kept many of us on the straight and narrow. Another of the messages that she had given to the children was that if Russia was not converted to the Catholic Faith, she would spread her evil ways throughout the world.

Fatima had a big influence on our religious beliefs. Although the apparitions at Fatima had occurred many years before, it was very real for us all, as one of the visionary children, Lucy, was still alive and well and was now a nun in a convent. My mother often encouraged us to pray for Sister Lucy.

During one of the apparitions at Fatima, we were told that Our Lady had given special messages to the children. One was a deep dark secret and it became known as the 'Third Secret of Fatima' We were terrified as to what that secret might be. The Pope of Rome and successive Popes were the only people who knew the secret. We all assumed that it contained the date for the end of the world. It was often said that the Pope would not reveal its content, as it would frighten half of the world to death. So if Russia and its Communist people were bad news, they mustn't have been as bad as the Protestants, or so we thought. After all,

Home Wasn't Built in a Day

we didn't pray for the conversion of the Protestants. They must have been beyond redemption. Well, that's how we saw it anyway!

A few times a year at the end of Mass I would be requested by the Priest to remain in the sacristy with my vestments on. Then, I would be asked to hold a lighted candle and a font of holy water and to go back out to the altar rails with the priest, where he would pray over a woman. This was known as churching. After childbirth, a woman could not go to any church services until she was 'churched' which, in essence, was the purification of her soul. If a mother gave birth to a child outside of wedlock, not alone was she the talk of the place, but the church would not allow her the opportunity of being 'churched,' thus she was forced to remain in her so called 'impure state.'

At home, we were never allowed to forget our Catholic faith. It seemed that troubled or not, everyone relied on religion and faith in God. People were very devoted to their Catholic faith and didn't take kindly to interference from different religions. At that time, the Jehovah Witnesses were always in town, trying to spread their beliefs. Hardly a week would go by without them calling to the door. They called to every house, and at every door they got the same frosty reception. Everyone believed that the Jehovah's were the devil's own patrons working for him on earth. We were always warned by my mother that whenever they called, they were to be told to go away and never to come back. In hindsight though, we all realised that these people were believers in the same God as ourselves, and that there was absolutely nothing evil or sinister about their missionary work.

Paddy Cronin

Sometimes my mother would cook bits and pieces of food on a small primus that burned paraffin oil. She would send me to Joe Naughton's at the corner for a half gallon of oil. On one particular day he said to me, 'Are you young Cronin from back the street?'

'I am,' I said.

'Good mind not to give you any oil.'

'Why?' I said.

'I'll tell you why' said Joe. 'Your father tried to give me a bad name.'

I wondered what all that was about. I went home and told my mother but all she said was to forget about it. I kept on, and on at her. 'Ah, come on, Ma, please tell me,' I said.

After my pestering and pestering her, eventually she told me. 'One night while Joe Naughton was in bed, your father painted 'The Clare Bar' on the wall of his house.'

In later years I discovered that the Clare Bar was the name of a promiscuous premises in Limerick.

Joe Naughtons's house was in the shadows of the once infamous Limerick Hellfire Club. A couple of hundred years previously, the Hellfire Club housed the most notorious hell-raising bucks in the area and catered for their every need. Many stories emanated from the club and were handed down through the generations. Within the Hellfire Club, everything that was considered sacred and solemn was ridiculed and treated with contempt. All the members were men, but ladies of the night were invited in on a regular basis. The order of the day consisted of heavy gambling, frequent orgies, black masses, mock crucifixions and banquets with heavy drinking.

Home Wasn't Built in a Day

Rumours were widespread that the Satanic Majesty himself was in attendance and that he would take the form of a black cat. Joe Naughton always had a black cat, and I thought it was a direct descendent of the cat in that infamous club. In the club, notorious members drank hot *scaltheen*, a mixture of whisky and butter, with which they then toasted Lucifer. People associated with the club carried a curse for years. The Fitzgerald family, long associated with the old castle of Askeaton and who were members of the club, carried that curse, so when John Fitzgerald Kennedy was shot in Dallas it was no surprise to the locals.

'Arah, what luck could they have?' said local saddler, Chris Casey, 'The devil's people have the devil's luck.'

After the story my mother told me about Joe Naughton, and my father painting the front of his house, I was never seen near his shop again.

The locality was well noted for its singing and dancing, which took place mostly in people's houses. My mother told me of great nights they had singing and dancing at Mac Carthy's house. There was one particular story about a character, whom I knew myself, called Mick Enright. One night at one of Mac Carthy's hooleys, he was playing on a comb with a piece of paper. This was an old and cheap traditional way of knocking out a tune. As Mick rattled out *Father Halpin's Top Coat* on the comb, one of the guests noticed that his privates were showing through a hole in his trousers. As the music stopped he was immediately confronted and asked, 'Mick, do you know your balls are hanging out?' to which he replied, 'You hum it and I'll play it!'

Paddy Cronin

The saying 'You can sing for it' took on a whole new meaning when Jim Slattery from The Lane went on a week end break to Tralee. Jim, who booked into the finest bed and breakfast in Kerry, was a great singer. In fact, it was often said that 'you would stand in the frost to listen to him.' At the time, it was traditional to pay the lady of the house for your stay on the morning that you were leaving for home. However, the night before Slattery was due to return home, he announced to the house that he would like to sing a song for the landlady. Jim duly rendered in his baritone voice, *Then You'll Remember Me*:

When other lips and other hearts
Their tales of love shall tell,
In language whose excess in parts
The power they feel so well:
There may, perhaps, in such a scene,
Some recollection of days that have as happy been,
And you'll remember me, and you'll remember,
You'll remember me!

Slattery brought the house down with his singing and immediately made for home. And, by God, was he true to his song! The following morning the poor old landlady lived to regret his operatic voice as he left her weeping for her money.

My mother used to tell us about another character who lived in the Lane just around the corner from us. His name was Mitchell Bradley. God, he was peculiar! He suffered from a rare form of speech impediment, in which he would constantly get his phrases and diction mixed up. Mitchell proclaimed, 'I was eating the mail

Home Wasn't Built in a Day

car when my breakfast went back. The door in bed and Maggie wide open.'

In hindsight, it might be considered that Mitchell had some unusual form of dyslexia, but at the time, people had no clue as to what caused his confused dialogue.

Tom Collins, who was better known as 'Tom the Saint,' proclaimed that he would be the next Pope of Rome. In the height of winter he would sleep outside in the open fields. This he did as penance for his sins, and the sins of the world. He would go to Mass on a daily basis and was often seen at the church with his clothes frozen to his body from a hard night's frost. Tom would walk up the church with hands joined proclaiming 'The Lord has appointed me as the next Pope of Rome'

It was well acknowledged that poor old Tom had taken his love of religion too far and that it was a major contributor to his unsteady state of mind.

Although he had the eyes of a hawk, Tom Mitchell applied for the blind pension. Tom was well known in the community for trying his luck at any potential government handouts. He was asked to attend the local library for sight assessment, but his application failed miserably. On entering the library, Tom was told to wait in the front room, which had a window overlooking the river and village. A stranger entered the room and Mitchell assumed that he was another applicant for the blind pension.

'Nice day,' remarked the stranger.

'Tis,' said Mitchell.

'God,' said the stranger as he looked out the window, 'isn't that a fine pony over there on the hill?'

Paddy Cronin

'Arah, Jaysus,' said Tom, 'That's no pony, that's Jack Cronin's ass. Shur, wouldn't I know him from the white head?'

'Well,' said the stranger, 'you can go and forget about the blind pension. I'm the assessor and you have better sight than myself.'

Early on Sunday morning's, my mother would ask me to go to John Joe Casey's shop to get the Sunday newspaper, *The Sunday Express*. Casey's ran a small shop selling newspapers and a few odds and ends and it was the only place in the village that you could purchase an English newspaper. My mother liked the English newspapers since the time my father used the send the odd one home in his parcels. Even in times of adversity and poverty, people never lost their wit or sense of humour. It was well said that when Mary Kate Sheahan ordered a toilet roll from John Joe and when he asked her what type she wanted, her answer was 'On the whole, it doesn't matter John Joe!'

There were plenty of toilet rolls but very few toilets in the locality. If one had an outside toilet they were indeed very privileged. Mrs Moore in The Lane had an outside toilet. She would keep lodgers. A Mr Mulcahy lodged with Mrs Moore for a very long time. He worked locally as an engineer for the Board of Works. One frosty winter's morning before he got up, he found the urge to go to the toilet. Rather than go out to the outside toilet he decided to deposit his business in a newspaper and duly put it under his bed. His intention was to dispose of it in the evening when he arrived back from work. However during the day the landlady, Mrs Moore paid a visit to his room and

Home Wasn't Built in a Day

to her horror found the newspaper and its contents under Mr Mulcahy's bed. She was extremely cross and decided to tackle Mulcahy when he arrived in the evening.

'Mr Mulcahy' said Mrs Moore, 'I saw something terrible in the newspaper this morning.'

Mulcahy replied, 'Well, Mrs Moore, I wouldn't believe everything you see in the newspapers.'

Mrs Nolan in Plunkett Road also kept lodgers for a living. She started this little business after her husband was tragically killed in the local lime factory. During one of the routine blasts quarrying the limestone, he was killed instantly by flying debris. Mrs Nolan's house gained a well-deserved reputation as being good digs. It had all the facilities that a lodger required at a time when lots of households had less than the bare essentials. Lots of her clientele were young bank clerks who had been posted to the local National Bank. In the mid-1960s a young banker from Newbridge, County Kildare lodged there. His name was Christy Moore, and once he finished work in the evening he was forever strumming his guitar. At the weekends, he would do the rounds of the public houses playing the guitar and singing folk songs. In 1966, there was a nationwide bank strike and Christy decided to travel over to England to earn a crust. He never returned to Askeaton, and never again worked in the bank. Christy Moore became one of Ireland's most famous folk-singers and has since graced the stage with endless chart hits for more than forty years.

If Mrs Nolan and the people of Plunkett Road were lucky enough to have a toilet, lots more of the other townsfolk were not. The river Deel, which flows through the village was rat infested. If you walked across the bridge and looked down on the water and river bank you would see the rats swimming and scavenging. The reason for this was because of the dumping of human excrement by local residents who didn't know any better or have any other way of disposing of it. There was no proper sewerage system in place so many people had no choice but to use the river.

On my way to Casey's shop for my mother's paper, the bell of the Protestant church would ring. The bell of this church had a different tone to the bell that rang in the Catholic Church. Firstly, it rang at ten o'clock, which for us was a very strange time, and secondly, nobody took any notice of it. The bell was a reminder to the Protestant fraternity that their service would begin in half an hour. Thomas Ryan, my cousin would meet me at the paper shop and on hearing the bell both of us would recite:

Proddy Waddy ring the bell,
Call the Proddy's down to hell.

You see, we were taught and firmly believed that all other religions, especially the Protestants, were destined to spent their afterlife in the company of Lucifer. At school we were warned to stay away from 'that place' and that if we went near the Protestant church while a service was in progress, we would have to receive special absolution from the Bishop.

Protestants, it was said, told their sins to the wall, and that was how they made their confession, so in one way we used to envy them. Telling their sins to the wall was a lot better than having to face a priest in the confessional.

Home Wasn't Built in a Day

Anyhow, we did our best to ignore their place of worship. The whole Protestant thing frightened us. I was always glad that I was fortunate enough to be born and baptised a Catholic. We used to say to each other at school, 'Who wants to be a Protestant anyway? They end up in hell'.

Well, that's what we believed, as it was driven into us by our teachers, priests and parents alike. The bottom line was that God was a Catholic, and there was no arguing with that.

One particular Sunday morning, bravery and curiosity got the better of us and Thomas and I decided to pay a visit to the Protestant church. We climbed a wall near the church and through an open window we listened to the service. We were eager to see and hear what all the so-called blasphemy was about. We stood on the wall for about two minutes. They were singing hymns, just like the ones we sang at our church.

After a couple of minutes, we ran off and pretty much immediately, guilt set in. We thought we had committed a mortal sin. I could not say a word at home about where we had been as my mother would have killed me. I could not sleep in bed that night because of the fear and guilt I was feeling. I cried and felt sorry for myself, because I had visions of the fires of hell, with me burning in them. I felt I had committed the ultimate sin, worse even than a mortal one. I had let everyone down; my late father; my mother; my sisters; my uncle the priest. I prayed to God for forgiveness and promised that I would never sin again. I must have said ten acts of contrition.

'Oh my God, I am heartily sorry for having offended thee . . .'

Paddy Cronin

I was sure that there was no way out of this one. I had brought indecency and disgrace to my family. At school the following day, I somehow was able to bring up the subject of the Protestant church. I was so relieved at the teacher's answer.

'It's no mortal sin' he said, 'if you did not actively take part in the service.'

'What does that mean?' I said.

'Well you would have to attend their service and do whatever they do,' said the teacher.

'Would listening at the door be a mortal sin, sir?' I asked.

'Probably not, Cronin,' he said, as he pulled tightly on his braces, 'but I sincerely hope you or any one of you down there would never do that.'

'Oh, no sir' I said, as the rest of the class nodded their heads in agreement.

Again I was so relieved. At least I did not have to seek absolution from the Bishop. I was definitely staying away from the Protestant church in future. I'd often wished that that bloody Protestant church was not there at all. It was too much of a temptation and some day I might go too far and end up committing a grievous sin and put the whole family to shame. That would be big trouble then, if I had to go to see the Bishop of Limerick and seek absolution. I came to the conclusion that the Protestants and their church were bad news.

I remember my father telling me that some years previous, when he was a young man, himself and a friend had attended a funeral of a Protestant in that same church. Like me, guilt had set in and he immediately

Home Wasn't Built in a Day

went to confession. The priest refused him absolution and instructed him to go and see the Bishop of Limerick immediately. He never told me if he carried out the priest's instruction or not. I imagine he probably said many many acts of contrition, rather than risk facing the irate Bishop, and confessing his so-called crime.

On another occasion, there was a funeral in the grounds of the Protestant church. One of their members was being laid to rest. Curiosity again got the better of a few locals and they climbed to the top of a tree just outside the church wall. The coffin was lowered down into the grave and the rector started to pray out loud for the soul of the departed, with his hands raised to the sky.

'May he rest in peace and may the angels come and raise his soul straight up to heaven.'

A voice from the top of the tree was heard saying; 'I'm forty feet higher than you and I've seen fuck all pass up yet, Amen.'

My mother told me of great hostility between the Catholic and Protestant churches when she was young. She spoke of the Catholic priest spitting out on the road when he would pass the Protestant minister. This was no longer the case when I was growing up, but there was certainly still a divide, which was purely as a result of fear of the unknown and complete ignorance about the differences in our religious beliefs.

When it came to courting couples, Protestant clergy were more tolerant and never bothered boys and girls who were out for a walk. Catholic priests, however, were different. They would poke the hedgerows and search the laneways for courting couples. They were known to beat the bushes with their walking sticks in search of what they called 'sinners of the flesh'. Young men and women were frightened to death of priests patrolling the hedgerows. The priests assumed that courting couples were impure and 'occasions of sin'. As far as most priests were concerned, they assumed the worst, in terms of sexual behaviour. Most of the time, these courting couples were just out walking and flirting in an innocent manner. One might wonder how the Catholic church, who promoted the family so much, ever expected young men and women to meet each other, get married and settle down.

THIRTEEN

'Is the boss in?' said the man with the unshaven face and pinstripe suit.

'Mama' I said, 'there's a man in the shop looking for the boss.'

'Oh, he's just one of them itinerants selling stuff,' she said.

'Hello Missus, we have lovely linoleum and the best of Axminster carpet; are you interested?'

'Arah, I'm not. Shur, I've no place to put it down anyway.'

'Will you sell us the jug inside the window so, Missus?'

'Oh God, no way, that was belonging to my late husband.'

'Well the Lord have mercy on him, Missus, I'm sure he has the light of God in heaven. Anything else so Missus?'

'I have a wireless,' my mother said.

'Not worth much, Missus, 'tis television that's all the go now. I'll give you half a crown for it.'

'Oh God, no way,' said my mother.

'Look, Ma'am, there's five shillings. Take it or leave it,' he said.

'Take it away' she said, 'but it breaks my heart to sell it.'

'May God increase you, Missus, and the light of God to all the souls.' said the itinerant.

That old wireless had brought us many happy memories. We'd wait patiently just before five in the evening to hear the introduction jingle to the tune of *O'Donnell Abu*. That meant that Athlone, which was Radio Eireann, was about to come on air.

'Tune in to Athlone,' my mother would say.

After turning on the wireless, it would take about three minutes to heat up. We listened to that old wireless with intense fervour. It had been a wonderful source of information. We had listened to Santa leaving the North Pole each Christmas Eve, and hurling matches on a Sunday when the great Micheal O'Hehir brought the action into the room. Our only wish as we parted with the wireless was that some day, we might be fortunate enough to have a television.

In any event, we had better than television at times, with the weekly antics of a couple living across the road from us. An English lady called Daisy Laing rented the house and she kept a lodger called Mr Fitzgerald. We would wait at our top window every Sunday night to watch and listen to the weekly ritual. Mr Fitzgerald would arrive back from the pub drunk and Daisy would have the door locked. She would be upstairs with the front window opened and shouting, 'Go away Fitzgerald, you're drunk!'

'Oh please Daisy,' he would say, 'let me touch you with my lips.'

Then the suitcase would fly from the top window

'Off with you, you drunk'

'God blast you, you bitch' he would shout.

'And fuck you, as well' Daisy would shout, in her English twang.

Then my mother would say, 'she must be low-class to use the soldiers' word. No woman uses the soldiers' word.'

We would ask our mother what was the soldiers' word.

'The 'F' word,' she'd say.

Finally Fitzgerald would burst into song, using his trump card, the one he knew would melt Daisy's heart.

If you were the only girl in the world,
And I were the only boy,
Nothing else would matter in the world today,
We could go on loving in the same old way.
A Garden of Eden just made for two
With nothing to mar our joy;
I would say such wonderful things to you,
There would be such wonderful things to do,
If you were the only girl in the world,
And I were the only boy.

Daisy would predictably fall for his charm and come down to let him in. It became obvious that Mr Fitzgerald was much more than just a lodger. When Daisy and Mr Fitzgerald vacated the house, it was taken over by Jack Shaughnessy and his new wife. The newlyweds were so different, two very gentle people. However, Jack liked a drop of whiskey and would over-indulge now and then. Mrs Shaughnessy did not like it when he had too much to drink and when he arrived back from the pub, she would refuse to speak to him. The following day Jack would be asked by his mates about how he got on with the wife after his few drinks. His response would always be, 'A beautiful picture, but no sound.'

As time went on, our little shop became a very viable business. Each Christmas, we would sell toys, which was very profitable and a huge attraction locally. I remember one Christmas Eve when I was about eleven, and my mother sitting on my bed at about two in the morning telling me that she had made £100 over the Christmas on toys. This was an enormous sum of money for us. All of this money was put away in the post office on Hansel Monday (the first Monday in January), for the benefit of her three children. She always told us it was deemed good luck to save on Hansel Monday, so if we had a few shillings to save after Christmas, we would wait until then to deposit them in the post office. The post office was where financial transactions took place for most people. Although there was a bank in the village, most people were never inside the door of it. The bank seemed to be for important people or people with lots of money, not for ordinary townspeople like us.

My mother always looked forward to New Year's Eve with great enthusiasm. I suppose she always hoped that the new year would bring in better luck than the one we were leaving behind. I often thought that she placed more emphasis on the new year than Christmas. Each New Year's Eve, close to midnight, lots of people from all over the parish would gather in the square and march through the streets playing music. It seemed as if every man, woman and child took part in the parade. My mother always insisted that we follow it, even for just a few steps. She would meet it as it passed our front door and together we would march with it down the street.

'Tis lucky,' she'd say, 'to follow the parade and place our good fortune for the year ahead in the hands of God.'

And then she'd say, 'That the coming year may be

Home Wasn't Built in a Day

better than the one that's gone, with the help of God, and His Blessed Mother.'

All of us children helped out, and the shop, was fast becoming a focal and meeting point for young people. Of course it was also good for business that there was always a crowd of young people about the place. My mother often referred to it as a great outlet and social place for people to meet. The rapport that she had with the customers, especially the young men and women, was very special. I guess she became the local match-maker; she liked to be considered that anyway, and she revelled in the role. Many a romance was founded at Cronin's shop. Young men from the local Aeroboard factory would meet there after work in the evening and usually have a bottle of Nash's lemonade or orange. Willie Murphy from Newcastlewest was the ladies favourite, as he was an extremely handsome young man. Pauline Mac Carthy, a young local girl, had a serious crush on Willie.

'Please, Mrs Cronin,' she said, 'make a date with him for me.'

'Call down tomorrow evening Pauline at half--five and he will be here and I'll fix you up. He'll be finished work then.'

Pauline arrived at five, all dolled-up. She was nervous, but very excited at the prospect of dating gorgeous Willie. Willie arrived in the door at half-five and when Pauline laid her eyes on him, she fainted on the spot. The excitement was just too much for her. After many cups of water, Pauline came round, but Willie had fled the scene. After all, a young man on the look out for a wife was none too impressed with a lady that might be out cold when he'd arrive home in the evening, tired and hungry after a long day's work. I think poor old mother failed with that one.

The evening shift in the Aeroboard factory would finish at twelve and lots of the young lads would call to the shop on their way home for a bottle of orange. They would often stay 'til three or four in the morning chatting with my mother. She would arrange dates, but sometime she would advise a young boy or girl to forget about the person they had their eye on. Before she arranged the date, she would always consult with both parties to see if they fancied each other. We were often woken up in our beds from the chatter and laughter in the shop underneath.

Late one night, I was woken up by noise and shouting in the shop. A terrible scuffle had broken out in the street between five or six young men. They had been chasing a badger through the streets and eventually captured and killed it. The badger had come from a field on the outskirts of the village. One of the young men involved in the brawl ran into my mother in the shop and begged her to come outside and deem that he was the person who killed the animal. The reason they were hunting the badger was that badgers were declared vermin at the time, and a reward of half-a-crown awaited anyone who brought a dead one to the Garda barracks. Times were tough, so a fight broke out among the gang as to who had killed the badger. My mother calmed down the men and she persuaded them that the young lad that ran into the shop was the owner of the badger. She knew that the young lad could do with the reward of a few shillings. Her verdict and judgement was accepted and well respected.

Home Wasn't Built in a Day

Each night the local parish clerk John Joe Hogan, who also ran a hackney business, would call for a packet of cigarettes. John Joe would always ask us a riddle before he left. 'Girls have it, boys don't and Miss Mulligan had it twice before she got married. What is it?' said John Joe.

'Don't know,' we'd say.

And he'd reply, 'The letter L.'

No matter now many times John Joe asked us this riddle we always thought that there would be a smutty ending to it, but there never was.

As the lime factory became more enterprising and viable, a new managing director was appointed. He was an Indian, called Mr Metta. Not very many people in the locality had witnessed a person from another culture so he was very much spoken about and commented upon. It had emerged that Mr Metta was a vegetarian, which was a very unusual practice in Ireland at the time. Meanwhile a local man, Mick Mahoney called to our shop for his usual packet of cigarettes and my mother mentioned to Mick how nice the new man in the mill was and that he was a vegetarian.

'Easy knowin' he's a vegetarian' said Mick 'with the colour of him.'

Mahoney did not know what a vegetarian was and seeing a man with such sallow skin must have, in his opinion, been as a result of some unusual behaviour.

Old Mick Mahoney was a character in every sense of the word. In a pub one evening, he was explaining to the lads about a new invention in Limerick city, called traffic lights. He said, 'When they are green the traffic keeps comin' and when they change to red it stops.'

Someone said to Mick, 'What if there is a funeral?'

Paddy Cronin

Mick replied with a puzzled look on his face, 'Oh, the lights change to black then'

One Sunday morning, a grand American gentleman came in to the shop. 'Top of the morning to you,' declared the bearded one to my mother.

My sister Breda then whispered to my mother, 'He's the famous American singer and actor, Burl Ives'

Burl Ives had bought a house in the locality in the mid-60s and was a frequent visitor to the area. All four of us wanted to serve the famous actor. It was near Christmas time, so he asked us where was the best place to buy a turkey. My mother told him where you could buy one, but he said that he wanted about thirty. After successfully purchasing the thirty birds, he distributed them to itinerants who were camped around the area. He was a kind man and did not seek the limelight.

There were quite a few itinerants, or tinkers as they were often referred to, camped in the locality at the time. They were very poor and the women would go from door to door in the village, sometimes with a child in their arms, begging for money or food. Sometimes an old tinker lady would call and read people's fortunes for a few pence. Many of her predictions came to pass, even though it was obvious to most people that her predictions were often so broad that they could have applied to half the country. Although they were poor, they were also very honest.

The men folk would also go from door to door offering to mend pots and pans. This trade was quite lucrative for them, as people did not have the money to buy new pots and pans whenever the old ones became damaged. These 'tinkermen' gave a great service back then. My mother

Home Wasn't Built in a Day

told us that they got the name 'tinker' from having the ability to work with tin. In fact, she would say that they were fine tradesmen, who had been evicted from their homes many years before, and had no choice but to take to the roads.

On one particular Friday evening, Seamus Ryan, who had been living abroad and who was home on holidays, called to our shop to tell my mother about his encounter on the Quay with the Naughton family. Seamus was walking down the Quay to greet and say hello to neighbours he hadn't seen since his last visit home, which had been a few years previous. Timmy Naughton saw Seamus and immediately beckoned him into his house.

'Have a look at this morning's newspaper' said Timmy, pointing to the Social and Personal column.

The announcement of the engagement of Noel Fitzgibbon, the local doctor was posted in the *Irish Independent*. It read that Noel had become engaged to Shamrock Hanley.

'Great' said Seamus, 'I am delighted for both of them.'

Then the voice of Timmy's wife, Maggie, rose from a corner of the dark kitchen,

'Trust a Fitzgibbon, marrying a cousin of Saint Patrick.'

The Fitzgibbons were highly thought of, not least Noel, the young local doctor. Maggie, though, was having none of that grandeur stuff.

Each Sunday morning my father's father, Grandad, would call to our house and reminisce with my mother on times past. They would often talk about old songs and my grandfather would rack his brain to remember the words. Before he would leave he would always sing *The Glen of Aherlow*.

Paddy Cronin

My name is Patrick Sheehan, and my years are thirty-four;
Tipperary is my native place, not far from Galtymore;
I came of honest parents, but now they're lying low;
Though many's the pleasant days we spent in the Glen of
   Aherlow.

Grandad would always tell us a story from long ago, like the one about Jim Finn. Jim Finn lived in a little house up the road and was known as a gross exaggerator, a man who found it almost impossible to tell the truth. He had two terrier dogs that he walked through the village each day. One morning Jim was walking down the street with no sign of a dog anywhere. Grandad met him and asked, 'Where are the dogs today, Jim?'

'Long story,' said Jim, 'I had a terrible night; they are both now gone.'

'What happened?' said Grandad.

'As you know they were very vicious dogs' said Jim, 'during the night they ate one another and all I was left with were two tails.'

We were sure that this story was untrue, not because it had come from Grandad, but because it had been told by the infamous Jim Finn. It was just another one of Jim Finn's 'tall tales.'

Grand National day was a big day in town and a busy day in the shop. Most people had a bet on the big race. It brought people out of their homes to place a bet at the local bookie. My mother would give us a shilling each to place a bet on the race. None of us had a clue about horses and betting. She would open the newspaper at the racing page, give us a pin, instruct us to close our eyes and prod a hole on the race list. Whatever horse we stuck

Home Wasn't Built in a Day

the pin in was the one that we would back. My mother did not mind us having the odd flutter on Grand National day as it was only ever a bit of fun, and after all it was only petty gambling anyway. The thrill of winning, even a tiny sum of money was always exciting.

Each Sunday my mother would do the 'Spot the Ball' in the English Sunday newspaper. A picture of a football match was published with the location of the ball removed. Entrants would put an x where they thought the ball was. She would then give me her entry and I would go to the post office to post it. Week after week went by, but she still did not win the £100 jackpot. Occasionally, a little disappointed, she'd say, 'You'll never get anything for nothin' in this life, only what you work hard for.'

Twice a year a priest from the Order of Saint Camilla's would call to collect the contents of a mite box which we had on the shop counter. His name was Father Mac Cormack. He had been coming for many years collecting on behalf of the order of Saint Camillas, patron Saint of the sick. My mother would always encourage people to put a copper or two into the box. She built up a great relationship with the priest. He became her friend and she was delighted to have a priest as a friend.

Then on one occasion when Father Mac Cormack was due, another man came instead.

'I was expecting Father Mac Cormack,' she said.

'Who?' said the priest,

'Father Mac Cormack.'

'We have no Father Mac Cormack in the Order.'

'But he collects the mite box here every six months,' she said.

– 158 –

'Ah,' said the priest, 'that's Brother Patrick Mac Cormack.'
'Covering up,' she immediately said
'Oh, I must have thought he was a priest.'

Father Mac Cormack or Brother Mac Cormack, was probably just very proud that my mother had addressed him as a priest. After all, priests and brothers wore the same garb, being attired in a black suit and a Roman collar. Next time when the mite box was due to be emptied, Brother Mac Cormack arrived and my mother continued to call him Father as this was what she had grown accustomed to. He collected the money on behalf of his order and was probably not concerned whether people thought he was a priest or a brother. His mite box was always full to the brim and he was always very praising of the generosity of the local people.

It was great fun if we were let stay up late at night to help in the shop. This would only happen at the weekends, as during the week we had to be up bright and early for school. This was also the time when the odd character would drop in on his way home from the pub.

I loved it especially when 'Mixer' Murphy would arrive. 'Mixer' was a big strong man who arrived from Dublin to work on the building of a runway at Rynanna. Yeh, that's the same 'Mixer' Murphy that used to bring my uncle Mikie to and from work at the airport. Before leaving the shop, the 'Mixer', who would be loaded to the throat with drink, would then burst into verse about a song from his hometown of Dublin.

Now here's a story that's bound to shock
It's all about a murder at the Ringsend Dock

Home Wasn't Built in a Day

The woman in question young Biddy Mc Grath
She murdered two sailors with the straps of her bra

With me touriah fall da diddle ah
With me touriah ouriah ouriagh

Hearing the word bra was outrageous and funny to a young lad like me. My mother was never far away to protect us from any unsavoury conversation or comments.

I was amazed when one evening I saw a man wearing an earring for the first time. To me, this was very strange, as I had only ever seen a woman wearing earrings before. The man in question was the well-known traveller and singer, Pecker Dunne. One evening he arrived in town, got out of a car beside our house and headed into Kennedy's pub nearby. After a half an hour or so, a big crowd gathered outside the pub to hear the Pecker playing the banjo.

As youngsters we never saw the inside of a pub. Public houses were for men only; women or children were not allowed – well, definitely not children, and a woman would be seriously frowned upon if she was seen inside a pub door.

On another evening, news spread throughout the village that the Dublin folk group, 'The Dubliners' were in town and singing in Collins' pub. All the women and children gathered outside Collins', listening to the songs and music. The group made an unscheduled stop, purely to refuel! It was not only fuel for their automobile either, but also for themselves. They had plenty to eat and plenty to drink, especially Guinness which they loved. Lots and lots of Guinness!. These were exciting times indeed.

FOURTEEN

One of the parish highlights each year was the annual mission. Priests from Limerick, the Redemptorist Fathers, would spend two weeks in the church praying and preaching for the redemption of all souls, living or dead. Limerick had a tradition of being a very pious and devout city. It had an Archconfraternity in honour of Our Lady, which had 8,000 male members and was the largest in the world. These men were obliged to attend a weekly meeting, receive Holy Communion once a month and to make a nightly examination of conscience.

Now it was up to the country men and women to examine their consciences during the two weeks designated to them by the missionary priests. Every man, woman and child attended the mission. One week was set aside for the women and children and the other week for the men. My mother insisted that, as a young boy, I qualified for both, so I had to attend the two weeks.

Fire and brimstone and the fear of God was hurled at everyone, especially during the men's week. 'Oh, the dangers of company keeping, the demon drink, purity, and remember everyone, the fires of hell.'

Home Wasn't Built in a Day

Then the greatest tongue lashing of all would be rendered with the seven deadly sins: pride, envy, wrath, sloth, greed, gluttony and lust.

You could hear a pin drop as the priest denounced the sins of society. Gluttony and lust were top of his list.

'The sin of gluttony is being committed every day and night in this community,' the priest would say.

'Gluttony is not just about eating too much, but also about the consumption of alcohol. Every time you get drunk, you commit the sin of gluttony.'

Cold-faced men looked to the ground or straight at the altar, afraid and embarrassed to look each other in the eye.

'The drunken man, spending his night in the pub and his wife and family at home, hungry; Do ye care?'

Then the dreaded lust would be accusingly thrust at the congregation.

'Oh, the lack of self-control and the practice of self-abuse is the destruction of the soul.'

What the priest meant by this, I hadn't a clue, but I knew it was something really bad when he preached about it with such venom.

'Respect for women, where is it? Respect for the inner sanctum, your own bodies. What about all those impure thoughts? What do they lead to? I know: self abuse and the destruction of the mind, body and soul. Then you come to the confessional and say you are sorry for committing this sin. Prove you are sorry! I still hear the same old story and see the same old faces.'

'And what about emigration? I'll tell you about emigration. Emigration to England has served us well, especially when families were hungry, but now we are seeing the darker side. It has opened up a world of filth and promiscuity. Give ye a few extra bob and the devil gets the better of ye. When ye arrive home, ye have to bring the filthy book. Oh, you're not a man unless you bring back the lowest deprivation of filth. Well, I'll tell you that the gates of hell are facing you, whether you bring or read that dirt that degrades women to the lowest form. Your body is a temple of the Lord, but you have chosen to destroy it. Catholics who persist in importing such matter are not worthy to receive the Sacraments.'

The priest would then reflect on past good practices, with many of the congregation heaving a sigh of relief at his change of emphasis.

'Let us recall some of those practices that existed in the community down through the years; for example, the *meitheal*, which was called on threshing day.'

The *meitheal* was a group of neighbours who would offer their services for free.

'The puddings and bacon that were sent to the neighbours when the pig was killed. And the big attendance at funerals. I'm glad to say that in country areas like here, people are still good at fulfilling obligations like these.'

Women were not free from the preacher's wrath either. On one particular Saturday night, during women's week, a group of ladies were noticed leaving the church before the proceedings were over. One of the Mission priests had them followed to see where they were going. It transpired that they had taken a bus to bingo in nearby Shanagolden. The following night there was fire and brimstone from the altar. Not alone did these women feel guilty, but they were now totally exposed for their so-called 'crime.'

Home Wasn't Built in a Day

Last, but not least, the priest would ask everyone to hold a lighted candle and renew their baptismal vows.

'Do you denounce Satan with all his works and prompts?'

'We do.'

You would hear a pin drop in the church. Bill Brien's reply would be heard above everyone else, with his exuberance in denouncing the devil. He was an old man of great faith and the mere mention of the devil would make his blood boil. His deep voice would echo round the church with great intensity.

'We do, we do, we do . . .' Bill would proclaim.

Outside the church, traders would set up religious stalls and each stall would be very busy. Everyone bought a holy scapular which was blessed at the mission and you wore it round your upper body, night and day, thereafter. The scapular was a cloth necklace that had a holy picture attached to it. It was specially dedicated to the Blessed Virgin Mary. My mother insisted on us all wearing a scapular. She said it would protect us wherever we went. I would never take off my shirt in summer in case my friends saw the scapular. It was embarrassing for a young lad of my age. I was only about eleven years at the time.

Holy pictures, Rosary beads and Saint Philomena's cord were also sold and blessed during the two weeks. The cord was a symbol of devotion to Saint Philomena and a sign of faith in her to protect your body and soul.

Contrition and the fear of God was in everyone's mind during these two weeks. Business was brisk at the stalls, so much so, that to buy something at one of the stalls, you would have to queue for ages. It seemed that everyone was turning over a new leaf.

Another religious occasion I fondly remember was the annual pilgrimage to Knock Shrine in County Mayo. It was here that the Blessed Virgin Mary was said to have appeared to a group of people in 1879. Aged about ten, I boarded the train in Askeaton with my cousin Mary Shanahan and her father Dave, who was our guardian for the day. The trip was booked a number of weeks in advance as it was a very popular excursion.

The journey to Knock was mostly spent reciting the Rosary, usually initiated by Dave Shanahan, and hymns in honour of the Blessed Virgin were sung by the local garda, John Kelly, respectfully known as Guard Kelly.

Our banner, declaring where we came from, was proudly displayed at the shrine, held aloft by a few old men. Mass was celebrated at the Holy Grotto and then we all went off to the many stalls to buy religious presents. The journey home I could never recall, as I always fell asleep from pure exhaustion.

On arrival at Askeaton railway station late at night, we were greeted by many of the pilgrims' families, eagerly awaiting their presents and wanting to hear about the holy site.

One particular pilgrimage I will always remember, was the excursion in 1965. There was more than a bit of confusion on our arrival home at Askeaton station. Last off the train, and lucky that he did not travel on to many more stations, was local character, Charlie Madigan. Charlie, as well as attending funerals, always made the pilgrimage to Knock. On this occasion though, he had taken a couple of pints of stout at Knock and had fallen asleep on the journey home. Our train was delayed on the way home as

Home Wasn't Built in a Day

on leaving Knock, Madigan could not be found. He was in a pub and eventually turned up a half hour late.

Guard Kelly declared, 'I don't ever want to see you on a pilgrimage to Knock again Madigan. You have no interest in Knock, just liquor, liquor, liquor.'

Madigan woke up and thought he was still in the pub and looked for the best man in the house to come outside the door; all five feet of him!

'God blast ye, the lota ye' said Charlie, 'there's no good in any of ye.'

I thought it very funny to see him wobbling his way home from the station, but I think I was the only one to see the funny side.

I often wondered whether I was religious or just frightened of death. Across the road from us was funeral undertaker, John Mac Knight. A couple of times a month, John would have a funeral to undertake. I was friendly with his son Seamus and once a funeral was announced, Seamus was given the task of lining the coffin and embossing the name plate, for the coffin. The coffins and accessories were stored in his grandmother's house, since she had passed on herself. Seamus would often ask me to help him. I would hold down the silky lace while he pinned it to the inside of the coffin. Many a time Seamus would ask me to lie in the coffin and test it for size. It was so eerie! I was scared of my life that he would put the lid on and screw it down.

Death never seemed to hold any great mystery for the majority of people. When Mary Sullivan's husband Paddy was dying, and on the last legs, she decided to have everything in order for his impending death. One of the

Paddy Cronin

first things she did, was to go into Canty's Drapery to buy a habit to have him laid out in.

'What price are the habits?' she asked the shop assistant, Tom Moran.

'Well,' said Tom, 'you have the basic one for five shillings, the next one for seven shillings, which, by the way, is made of a stronger material, and the top of the range one which comes with cap, gown and socks for ten shillings.'

'I'm not sure which one to take,' said Mrs Sullivan, 'to me 'tis all much of a much-ness. Arah Mr Moran, I'll go with the basic one for the five shillings' she said.

Tom Moran then replied, 'I'll have to warn you Mrs Sullivan, if you go with that one, it's very possible that he will have the backside worn out of it in a week or two.'

Mrs Sullivan, however, stuck to her guns and purchased the basic five shilling habit, reckoning she could make better use of any additional money herself, rather than wasting it on a fancy habit for her deceased spouse. After all, where Paddy Sullivan was going, he wasn't going to be bothered if the habit fell to bits after seven days or seven years.

Throughout my youth, Saint Patrick's Day was only commemorated in a religious way. There were no parades or pageants – well, at least not here in our village anyway. My strongest recollections were of picking shamrock about a week before the feast day. My mother would then send it to relations across the water in England.

The day itself was a holy day of obligation, so the church was always packed to the rafters. All the adults wore huge sprays of shamrock and the children wore green badges. Once Mass was over, the children would go off

Home Wasn't Built in a Day

to play, and the men would retire to the pub to 'wet the shamrock.' The sprays of shamrock would wilt over the course of the day, and when it was time to go home to the wife, there was usually nothing left of the once glorious display. Saint Patrick's Day was traditionally the only day during Lent that one could have a drink, as most men gave up the bottle for their Lenten sacrifice. Signs on, when Paddy's Day arrived, it was one worth celebrating.

August 15th, the feast of the Assumption, was deemed a holy day by the Church calendar. We had to attend Mass as if it was a Sunday. This day was not like any other holy day as it was also the feast of Barrigone Well, which was dedicated to the Blessed Virgin Mary. We knew therefore that our mother would be trying in every way possible to have us all make the short pilgrimage. The well was about four miles away and all four of us would walk there. My mother had told us that if we saw a little fish swimming round the well, any wish that we had would be granted. Looking for that fish was the only thing that encouraged us to go to that well. Needless to say, none of us ever managed to see it!

A huge trail of people would walk around the well slowly, reciting the Rosary. For me and my two sisters, apart from being tired from the long walk, the endless chanting of prayers over and over was seriously boring. We never shared our feelings with our mother and endured the ritual, as fervently as children could. By the time we got home, exhaustion had consumed us and we were all fast asleep before our heads had hit the pillow.

FIFTEEN

As in any community, and especially in the sixties, sport played a big part in everyday life. I was a soccer man. That meant that I could not play hurling or football without denouncing the foreign game. The GAA enforced ban meant that you played national Gaelic games only, and if you played soccer or rugby, known as foreign games, you were banned from the GAA.

Mick Mackey, the great Limerick hurling legend was pictured in the national papers at a soccer match in Cork. This made huge headlines; a great Gael at a foreign game. Surely this man warranted expulsion from the Gaelic Athletic Association? Well that's what all the observers thought back then. It was well said at the time though, that the reason he was there was to act as an observer, and report back on any fellow Gaels who were in attendance. My friends and I were caught on many occasions in the GAA field kicking football, from where we were duly escorted, being accused of not rising the ball to our hands, which in turn meant that we were playing soccer.

'Get out of here with yer foreign game,' we were told. 'Next time the Guards will be called.'

Home Wasn't Built in a Day

'We were playing Gaelic football,' we'd say.

'Ye were not. We have been watching ye for the past half hour and not once did ye rise the ball. Off with ye, off with ye, ye traitors, gobshites and gombeens'

They would rant and rave that we had desecrated their 'sacred ground' and made it into a 'den of iniquity'.

Our escorts were not always polite or courteous either, as the proverbial kick up the behind was more often than not applied. We would be escorted out in single file from the field. You did your best to avoid the back of the queue, as that person would be the most likely one to get the kick up the rear end. We never resisted the eviction and accepted our punishment as gracefully as humanly possible. I certainly never mentioned to my mother about our confrontations with the GAA authorities, as I would have got very little sympathy and probably another clip around the ear for my defiance. In hindsight, the Gaelic people or 'Gaels' as we referred to them, were just protecting their sporting organisation like any other club or society. Unfortunately, we could only see it as an 'us and them' situation, with 'us' usually ending up feeling annoyed and bitter.

I grew up appreciating the game of soccer, playing it to the best of my ability, which was at a very modest level. I must say that I admired the soccer mentors, especially the big man, John Joe, who brought me to the field every week to learn the game and acknowledged what sport was all about. The big man would collect me at our front door and carry me on the bar of his bike. On the way, lots of children would join in and follow us all the way to the soccer field. He was like the 'Pied Piper.' I did not have

Paddy Cronin

football boots, but John Joe always managed to have a pair for me. Mind you I was not alone there. Most of the kids struggled to have football gear, but John Joe always did his best to kit us out. The football boots were like hobnail boots, covering my ankles as well as my feet. I was a really terrible player as a young lad. The boys around me would shout, 'Go for the ball Cronin, don't be afraid of it'

Well, if the truth was known, I was frightened of my life of it. The balls in those days were very heavy, not even totally round and had a very rough lace which fastened the leather around the inside bladder. When it was wet it was almost impossible to kick it without hurting your feet or toes. Heading the ball too was a nightmare as such a heavy sodden ball made it very painful.

Our village was a Gaelic stronghold, but it also had a very strong rugby background. This, I think, made the rift between the Gaelic games and the so-called foreign games even greater. The people with the rugby background invariably played soccer. In 1941 the local rugby team won the Transfield Cup which was a huge feat. I think that this may have contributed to the divide that existed, in that a lot of young men were drawn towards the rugby and soccer after that.

It is said that sport is a great leveller and that it brings communities together; sadly it divided many a neighbourhood at the time. The GAA were also very much affiliated and promoted by the Catholic church. After all, it was and still is our national sport which evokes patriotism. Every priest in every parish had some affiliation to Gaelic games. I cannot ever recall though, seeing a priest at a soccer match in those days. Their presence was reserved strictly for Gaelic games alone.

Each year, without fail, Mac Fadden's Travelling Show would come to Askeaton for a couple of weeks. The church approved of the travelling shows, which they saw as an innocent form of entertainment, unlike that of the dancehalls that encouraged 'sinful' behaviour. Father O'Dea would often attend the shows, but we never knew if he was there for the pure enjoyment of it or to keep an eye on the proceedings.

The shows were entertainment at its best. Music, song and drama was brought to a rural community who appreciated each performance. Mac Fadden's also ran a local talent contest with a bottle of whiskey going to the winning performer and five shillings to the runner up. At one particular contest in the mid-1960s, the contestants were John 'Salt' Hanley, Paddy Leahy and Paddy Hart. John 'Salt' Hanley's entry was a recitation on the scourges of the demon drink. John 'Salt' liked his pint and a few whiskeys if the prize money somehow came his way. However, John had recently gone to the local parish priest and said that he now had decided to give up the drink.

'I want to take the pledge, Father. D'oul drink has me killed.'

'Good man John,' said the priest, 'stay away from it for a month and call back to see me then, and we can arrange about the pledge.'

John maintained that proclaiming his temperance pledge in public was proof to all that a new image was about to resurrect. He was easily recognisable as he was always picking up empty cigarette boxes from the pavements. It

Paddy Cronin

was said that he found £5 in a cigarette box many years before. John lead the life of a vagabond even though he had farming land in nearby Shanagolden which he had rented out. He was noted for going to the local butchers and asking them for meat, especially liver which had gone off. This, of course, he got for nothing. He would then bring it to my grandmother on the Quay, and ask her to cook it for him.

'God John I can't cook that, 'tis gone off.'

'Arah fuck it' said John, 'put plenty of salt on it.'

His tolerance of large quantities of salt earned him the nickname, John 'Salt'. John also had what many people referred to as a 'Map of Ireland' on his nose. These were blotches of red, resulting from the ravages of drink.

In Mac Fadden's talent competition, Paddy Leahy sang *The Rose of Tralee* and Paddy Harte, who was favourite to win the competition, sang *If those lips could only speak*. Out of pure devilment, Chris Nash campaigned the audience not to applaud Paddy Harte. There was complete silence when Harte finished his song and rapturous applause for 'Salt' and Leahy. John 'Salt' won the contest with Paddy Leahy in second place. Paddy Harte felt very hard done by and he vowed never to sing again.

'I have never been more insulted in my whole life. Here I am, a man who sang with the great Christy Lynch of Rathkeale and a man who has spoken to the late great John Mc Cormack, but this is the end for me,' said a demoralised Harte.

Then John 'Salt', as the winner of the competition, took to the stage again, bowed to the crowd and once again recited his poem.

Home Wasn't Built in a Day

*One night when I got frisky
Over some poteen whiskey,
Like waves in the Bay of Biscay,
I began to tumble and roar.
My face was red as a lobster,
I fell and I broke my nob, Sir
My watch was picked from my fob, Sir -
Oh, I'll never get drunk anymore!*

*Now I'm resolved to try it,
I'll live upon modern diet;
I'll not drink, but deny it,
And shun each alehouse door.
For that's the place, they tell us,
We meet with all jovial good fellows;
But I swear by the poker and bellows
I'll never get drunk anymore*

He was presented with the bottle of whiskey and spent the night on the street singing the praises of alcohol. That was the end of John's temperance and his pledge to forego alcohol in the future.

Gazette's cinema, which had established a permanent home in Askeaton in the early sixties, was a favourite haunt for courting couples. The cinema was like a tent, which was assembled and disassembled fairly easily, as the family used to move from town to town, staying in each place for a few weeks at a time. They eventually decided to remain permanently in Askeaton.

With lights out and the projector showing the film, the frolics would begin. Many couples would cuddle up with the frequent squeal from a woman, 'Take your hand away from there you dirty fella.'

Paddy Cronin

Then, it was lights on and the film would temporarily stop. Nora would then announce over the loudspeaker, 'Once more lads and you're out on your ear'

After an uncomfortable silence, the lights would once again be turned off and the film would recommence.

The one abiding memory of Gazette's is that whether you could afford the entrance fee to the pictures or not, nobody was ever turned away from the door. In the early fifties *The Quiet Man* was shown. The film proved to be a big hit at the box office, at home and abroad. The fact that John Wayne and Maureen O' Hara epitomised the perfect Irish couple gave the film huge appeal in Ireland, and every cinema-goer made it their business to see what turned out to be one of the best Irish films ever made. Its popularity in Askeaton ensured a full house each night for two weeks, an unprecedented attendance for any film ever.

SIXTEEN

On May 5th 1966, I was confirmed by the Bishop of Limerick, Dr Murphy. I have very few memories of the actual day, as apart from the spiritual aspect, it was more or less a non-event. There were no new clothes for the Confirmation. Luckily enough though, my mother had managed to buy me my first real suit the previous Christmas. I had worn it a few times since the Christmas and on one of those occasions, I fell and ripped the knee right open. My mother managed to have it invisibly mended, but you could still clearly see the spot where it was darned. Mrs Mac Carthy in St Mary's Terrace was the dear old lady that mended the pants. She was a dressmaker, and was one of a multi-talented family. It was at her house that my mother attended the dances long ago. The Mac Carthys were also very talented musicians, bakers and steeped in the local tradition of fishing. My mother also managed to buy me a new pair of shoes for the occasion. She sent me down to the local draper, Michael Collins, for a pair of 'squadron shoes'. Squadron shoes were in vogue at the time. There was an advert constantly on the wireless about them: 'Squadron are the shoes for me, the shoes with the six-month guarantee' It

Paddy Cronin

was very much hoped that I would get a lot longer than six months wear out of the shoes.

My mother saw the Confirmation as more of a spiritual event rather than anything else – well, spiritual for me in that I was receiving another one of the seven Sacraments of the Church. On Confirmation Day I walked back to church with some other lads who were also receiving their Confirmation. My mother had given me a shilling to have my photograph taken. We were told at school that a photographer would take photographs of us after the ceremony.

Funnily enough, my strongest memory of Confirmation was the fear of the slap that the Bishop would give me on the cheek. For months beforehand, I would ask my elders how hard and rough was the bishop's slap on the cheek. Of course, they wound me up by saying 'twas tough and rough. 'I was floored at the rails,' Mikie John O'Donoghue told me.

The Bishop called to the school a few weeks before the big event and he asked each one of us a religious question. I was worried that I would be unable to answer the question that he would ask me. The rumour went out that a young lad from the town of Rathkeale was asked to sing *Faith of Our Fathers* by the Bishop, and when he failed, the Bishop refused to confirm him.

Bill Mac Carthy's mother was taking no chances, so she marched him into the Redemptorists Fathers Archconfraternity in Limerick city for a whole month, so that he would learn every possible hymn. While all of us were out playing cowboy and Indians, poor old Bill was being driven to the city by the local taxi man, John Mac

Home Wasn't Built in a Day

Knight. The teacher said that if we were unable to answer any question put to us by His Lordship, we were deemed not suitable to be confirmed. For months beforehand, we learned off what seemed to be every question and answer in the Catechism. The Catechism was probably the most important book we had at school. Knowing all of the Ten Commandments was of the utmost importance..

'What's the Sixth Commandment, Lynch?'

'Thou shalt not commit adultery, sir'

'And you Cronin, what's the First Commandment?'

'First, I am the Lord thy God and thou shalt not have strange Gods before me, sir.'

I knew mainly that this meant staying away from the Protestant church. Well, it was driven into us that their God was a different one to ours. Anyhow, the Bishop, Dr Murphy, arrived. The big man who had been painted as a monster was in fact a very gentle man. He then started the questions. John O'Brien was first.

'Who made the world, my son?' said Bishop Murphy.

'God made the world, my Lord,' said John.

'Good man,' said the Bishop as he laid a gentle hand on his head.

God, I thought, all the easy questions first.

Then he came to me.

'Where are you from young man?'

'Askeaton, my Lord,' I said.

'Good man' said the Bishop.

I was so relieved. I was not even asked a proper question. My only concern now was the actual day and the smack on the cheek. In truth, the smack was as gentle as the questions he had asked us in the school.

Paddy Cronin

There was one question though, that caused me a lot of bother. A few weeks before the Confirmation, the teacher asked us to choose a Confirmation name. This would be another name that we would take in addition to our christening name. We were also asked to bring in our baptismal certificates to school. This presented me with a huge problem. I had been christened Patrick Joseph but my baptismal cert said Patrick Marian. This came from the religious influence of my parents, and in particular my mother. I was born in 1954 which was declared by the Church as 'The Marian Year,' so it was decided that I should be baptised Patrick Marian, rather than my registered birth name of Patrick Joseph. I was embarrassed out of my mind with the name Marian, a girl's name. I told the teacher that my name was Patrick Joseph and that I was taking the name John for my Confirmation. I also said that my mother had searched the house high up and low down for my baptismal certificate and there was no sign of it. I told him that she had found my birth certificate though, and eventually he agreed that this would be acceptable. Thank God I had managed to find an excuse to cover up what I perceived to be my terrible secret. How on earth could I face the rest of the class with a name like Patrick Marian?

Although Confirmation, on the whole, was a reasonably big event, especially the preparation at school, in 1966 it was overshadowed by the preparation for the commemoration of the 1916 Easter Rising. Most of the school year was taken up preparing and rehearsing for the fiftieth anniversary of the Rising. We were constantly reminded of how Padraig Pearse, James Connolly and their followers fought for Irish freedom by leading a revolt against the British forces. We were even brought on a school tour to Connemara to visit Pearse's cottage. We sang nationalist songs at school each day until we knew them off by heart.

The highlight of the year was a special ceremony in the school yard with Seamus Mac Knight reading the Proclamation of the Republic of Ireland, mimicking the oration given by Padraig Pearse during the famous insurrection. The spectacle then moved to the village square where Pat Wallace, who was later to become head of the National Museum of Ireland, read the Proclamation as well. This was a huge honour for these two boys. The intention of our teachers was that as young Irish men and women, the hair should stand on the back of our head with pride. They certainly achieved that! For once, even religion took a back seat.

One summers evening in 1966, I was sure that I was about to have a meeting with the Man above! I was swimming in the local pool and got into extreme difficulty. When the summertime would come round, my mother would persuade me to head off to the local swimming pool. I was not a very strong swimmer but always up to devilment. On this particular evening, I decided to swim the length of the pool for the first time and half way through I suffered a cramp and sank to the bottom. When I came to the top I cried for help. My friends were there but they ignored me. They thought that this was another Cronin prank. I went down a second time and I thought that this was the end for me. Again, I came to the top, and managed to grip onto a ledge. I swallowed what seemed

Paddy Cronin

like buckets of water. This was a very close shave with death. I wondered how many lives would have changed if the worst had happened. I must have said a hundred Hail Mary's when I got back on dry land. Thank goodness I was spared by the Man above!

During the 1960s, Teddy Boys ruled the streets of Limerick City. Well, it seemed like that anyway. It was fashionable for young men to dress in dapper suits with pointy shoes and have their hair combed back with lots of hair oil. We were warned about Teddy Boys who hung about street corners, as it was well said that they carried pen knives and were not afraid to use them.

Rather than the Teddy Boy look, I wore a Monkee hat. The Monkee hat was all the rage in the mid 1960s. It was made popular by the pop group, The Monkees. Every Saturday evening at six o'clock, the Monkees had their own half hour programme on Irish television. We still did not have a TV at home so I used to go to Sheahan's across the road to watch it. One member of the American pop group, Mike Nesmith, sported a knitted hat which became very popular. One man in town forever wore the great Monkee symbol. Tom Mangan sported the cap like young men wear the replica jerseys of their favourite football team today. Tom was like the representative of the Monkees here in Askeaton. The Monkees were real pop idols who set trends in fashion and music. The fact that television was relatively new and they had their own show, meant that they became very real, making them even more popular than the Beatles.

In June 1967, my uncle Jim, the priest, who was a teacher at Rockwell College in County Tipperary, informed my mother that he would be taking me to Rockwell College boarding school for my secondary education. My leaving for Rockwell created a big upheaval and had a profound effect on all the family.

I remember my first day leaving home in mid-September 1967, saying goodbye to my friends, especially my friend Declan Mac Daid, who had moved to the locality about five years previously from Donegal. Michael Sheahan from across the road came in to make sure that I was smartly dressed and ready for the road. I found it to be a very sad moment saying goodbye to my mother and sisters.

My auntie Katie brought me to Rockwell and I remember my first night crying myself to sleep. It was my first time ever being away from home. The first six months were the most difficult as home visits were very infrequent. After that, I settled down quite well.

Spending five years in Rockwell, albeit away from home for long periods, was enjoyable. It was wonderful participating in so many different games. Also there was no interference from any governing body as to which sport we played; not like the GAA ban which affected me at home. At Rockwell, we all played rugby, soccer and Gaelic games using the same playing pitches.

Each Easter, we would have about two weeks holidays and 'twas great to return home and meet my friends. I was also ordered by my mother to attend the annual Redemptorists men's retreat in Limerick. The retreat began on a Friday night and we were not released until Monday morning. Worse still, we were compelled to spend the entire weekend in total silence. For a young teenager this was difficult, but I treated it as part of my redemption.

Simon Lenihan from up the road was also a regular at the retreat. Simon was a few years older than me, but he claimed that he used the opportunity to his advantage.

'I can't wait for the retreat every year,' he said,

'I never thought that you were as religious as that Simon,' I said.

'Religious? Not me,' said Simon.

'So, why do you love the retreat Simon?' I said.

'Well, they won't allow me go dancing at home, so when everyone is tucked up in bed in the retreat house on Saturday night, I leave through a window and go to the Jetland ballroom. Great birds there too!'

Well, now that's an idea I thought, but it was only all in my head, as I was never brave enough to escape from the Retreat House.

My first summer home from Rockwell, in 1968, was very special. It was difficult being away from home for so long, so it was a holiday that I really looked forward to.

Prior to coming home, my mother had secured a summer job for me at the local lime plant. My position was that of messenger boy, cycling a bike here and there doing messages for the company management. I would collect mail at the post office, go to the shop for tea and milk, and on Saturdays answer the phone in the office. Nobody worked on Saturdays, so I would take phone messages and pass them on to management on the Monday. It was a very enjoyable job. I felt like a man, even though I was only fourteen. I was paid £3 10 shillings a week, which was considered huge money at the time.

During that summer, I spent all of my spare time on the local river, fishing for trout and poaching the odd

Home Wasn't Built in a Day

salmon. I also had wonderful fun, stroke-hauling grey mullet. Mullet would not take a bait legally, so an illegal method of foul-hooking them was practised by everyone. The bait consisted of a treble hook, with a lump of lead underneath the hook, which you dragged across the river. This was the stroke-haul. The same method was used to illegally catch salmon.

The water-keepers, who were known as bailiffs, would patrol the rivers trying to catch poachers taking the salmon. I was well-known to them as a poacher, but they could never catch me red-handed. My uncle the priest, who was a master fisherman, told me that there was nothing illegal about poaching mullet as it was done in tidal water. Mullet would come in from the Shannon estuary in the tide. He claimed that, once the tide was in, the Fishery Board had no rights on the water. Everyone who was interested in fishing, would spend many an evening stroke-hauling mullet and would sell their catch to the local fish monger, Chris Nash. Chris had a fish stand in a little corner of the village and he sold the mullet on as rock salmon.

'Fresh rock salmon,' Chris would shout at the oil lorries on their way to Foynes port, and he had plenty of takers, too.

He was also a very witty man. Mrs Dillon called to his stall one Friday for sixpence worth of fish.

'Is your cat sick, Ma'am?' Chris asked her.

Of course, no one, not even Mrs. Dillon, was ever offended by Chris's witty comments.

The custom of not eating meat on a Friday was very traditional in our community. Although the Church had lifted its ban on the eating of meat on a Friday, nevertheless, many households continued with the tradition. Lots of people were convinced that the Church had got it wrong by lifting the rule; in a funny way people saw the eating of fish as a penance for their sins. Unwittingly, it could be said that they were actually taking great care of their health with their weekly penance.

One Sunday evening in August of that same year, my cousin Thomas and I decided to go to a stretch of the river known as Gurt. The tide was in and the place was full of mullet. We started stroke-hauling and landed a few mullet. Then, out of the blue, a bailiff called Sean Benson jumped out of the bushes and demanded that we hand over all our fishing gear.

'For what?' we said.

'For illegal fishing' he said.

Then we quoted the law as we saw it – tidal waters, etcetera – but he was having none of it. He again asked us to hand over our gear, but we refused. He then said that he was summonsing us on two counts, illegal fishing and obstructing a water-keeper in his course of duty. Both of us ran home bawling our eyes out. About two weeks passed, and a man from Rathkeale called to our house and issued my mother with a summons to appear at Askeaton court in mid-September. As I was a fourteen year old minor, it was my mother's responsibility to appear on my behalf, so she had to attend the court, not me.

At least I could go back to Rockwell. I could never breathe a word to anyone at College. It would not be becoming of a Rockwell College student to have any altercation with the law. My mother was left to deal with the situation and to clean up what seemed to be a terrible

Home Wasn't Built in a Day

mess. Anyhow, the court came about and Benson the water-keeper swore that there was a run of salmon in the river on the night he caught us. Never in a month of Sundays would you have salmon moving in the tide. The judge would have had no idea of this, neither would my mother. Maguire, the judge imposed a fine of 10 shillings and ordered that all my fishing gear be removed from our house immediately.

My mother mustered up the ten shillings but she cried bitterly about the confiscation of the fishing gear. Some of the fishing gear at home belonged to my late father and it broke her heart at the prospect of handing it over. The police were summoned to call to our house and take the fishing gear, but luckily enough a young Garda called Malachy Keaveney only took a token old fishing rod belonging to me. He had a heart and he knew how unfair the whole situation was.

The following summer, when home from Rockwell, I was up to my same tricks, poaching the odd salmon. I was too wily for the bailiffs and they could never catch me. Mind you, at that time every fisherman was up to a bit of mischief.

One particular morning I ventured up the river for a bit of legitimate trout fishing but caught nothing. I decided to come home and on my way I stopped on the town bridge to talk to my friend Jim Casey. We spoke about fishing and how they weren't biting. Then a car pulled up on the bridge and the occupant asked me to hand over my rod. This man was a fella called Breen, who was head of the Limerick Fishery Board. I asked him why, and he said that I was standing on a Fishery Bye-Law with a mounted rod in my hand. A Bye-Law was an area where you were not allowed to fish. I said to Mr Breen that I was not fishing there. He acknowledged this, but said that the fact that I had a mounted rod, showed my intentions were not good. Learning from my previous experience, I handed over my rod. Again, being a minor, my mother was summoned to court and fined. The fine this time was fifteen shillings, as I had had a previous conviction.

During our poaching days, one of the biggest crimes ever committed occurred in Casey's house at around midnight one summer's night. A group of three or four of us were poaching salmon in an area of the river known as the 'Mill Hole', when suddenly, out of the undergrowth, came a number of bailiffs who had been watching our antics. We scampered off and ran in the back door of Casey's house which was near that particular area of the river. The bailiffs were not familiar with our route so we effectively lost them. We entered Casey's house, which always had its doors unlocked and was in complete darkness. Mrs Casey, who was upstairs in bed, could hear the noise down stairs and shouted down, 'Is that you Mike?' thinking it was her son Mike.

She got no response and fearful that intruders had entered the house, she immediately came to the landing and put on the light. Tommy Doupe who was part of our group immediately tried to turn off the light and pressed on what he thought was the light switch. What he actually pressed on was the holy water font on the wall. The holy water font fell to the ground and smashed into many pieces. We made for the front door and out onto the street. Alas, poor Tommy was left face-to-face with Mrs Casey, with the holy water font in smithereens on the floor. An unforgivable crime and a huge embarrassment.

The barber's shop, where I would go about once a month for a haircut, was no ordinary barber's shop, nor was the proprietor himself, Paddy Ryan. Paddy was as bald as a coot, but always sported a toupee. He maintained that it was not becoming of a respectable barber to be bald. Affectionately known as 'the Barber', our Paddy was a man of many words. One to always defend his sod, I once remember sitting on the bench of his shop waiting for my turn to be chopped, when a Yank dropped in for a haircut.

'Small place you have here' said the foreigner.

'Tis the finesht,' said the Barber.

'Where I get my hair cut in the States, we have a boulevard that has one hundred shops and a choice of twenty barbers.'

The Barber was having none of his bull.

'By God,' he said, 'we have a town not far from Limerick and it has a bridge six miles long.'

He was referring of course to the village of Sixmilebridge in County Clare. I think that shut up the old Yank for a while.

It seemed as though every character from the village congregated in the Barber's shop on Saturday mornings. Not all men were there for a haircut or a shave, but to catch up on all the local gossip and to have a good old natter. Old Joe Madigan, with his bent back and his head almost meeting the ground, was always clutching his Rosary beads praying for the grace of God. Sometimes that was more than justified, as the Barber's hands may not have been that steady from a whiskey or two the

Paddy Cronin

night before. One Saturday morning, the banter and chat took the usual twist.

'And there you have it, boys,' said the Barber, 'Buzz Aldrin and the Yanks on the moon.'

He was referring of course to the Americans' first landing on the moon in July 1969.

'Arah, Buzz my arse,' said Jim Clifford.

'They no more landed on the moon no more than the Man-in-the-Moon. I saw the whole thing on the television in Mac Donnell's pub last Sunday night. A bloody fake! Shur they can do anything with that television thing now.'

'Bigobs, you could be right' said Joe Madigan.

'I know I'm right,' said Clifford. 'They'd be better off minding the Mass than puttin' lies and dirt on that bloody screen.'

Paddy Mac Knight, who was a respectable man that had fallen on bad times, arrived at the shop. Paddy was a seasoned traveller, who trekked the country on his bike, and the ravages of time had somewhat distorted his mind. He was always dressed in black and could easily be mistaken for a priest. He claimed that his suit was of the finest material, tailor-made by the Danus Clothing Company in Limerick. In truth, he acquired his clothing from priests on his travels throughout the countryside. He would stop off at priests' houses and they would donate old clothes to him. Mac Knight's opening remarks when he entered the Barber's shop were, 'God bless ye all and may all the saints of heaven pray for yer souls, Amen.'

'Oh, Jaysus' says Clifford, 'Moon Man himself.'

'I"ll sing a song,' said Mac Knight 'in honour of the Man-in-the-Moon.'

'Spare us' said Clifford, 'just have your shave.'

The Barber shaved Mac Knight, and when he finished, Mac Knight said, 'That'll be two shillings, Paddy.'

The kindness of the Barber had no boundaries, so instead of charging Paddy Mac Knight for the shave, he paid him the two shillings.

'I'd have given him the County Clareman's payment, Paddy' said Clifford.

'And what's that?' said the Barber.

'The Lord spare you your health,' said Clifford, 'and tell him go his road.'

Poor old Mac Knight left and we could hear his tuneless voice echoing down the street. He was trying to mimic a tenor but his voice was more like that of a dying crow as he sang *The Moon Behind the Hill*.

I watch'd last night the rising moon,
Upon a foreign strand;
Till mem'ries came like flow'rs of June,
Of home and father-land;

I dream't I was a child once more,
Beside the rippling rill;
When first I saw, in days of yore,
The moon behind the hill.

The night they landed on the moon, every man, woman and child in the community sought out a television to witness the big event. With such a scarcity of televisions in the village, it meant the houses that had one were packed to the gills. I watched it at Michael 'Washington' Sheahan's house. His little front room was full of excited

Paddy Cronin

curious people, who when the big moment arrived, all stood to attention, with Washington fervently playing his tambourine for about five solid minutes. This was his salute. It was funny in one sense, everyone standing to attention and Washington bashing the living daylights out of his tambourine, or *bodhrán* as it was more usually known. It was as if we all had achieved something, not just the Americans! With the echoing sound of the drum, we were more like a primitive tribe from Africa, than people celebrating the landing of the 'Man-on-the-Moon'.

Then, without any counsel or warning Michael Sheahan gave his favourite recitation; all four-hundred-and-thirty-two lines of one of Limerick legendary poems, The Bard of Thomond's, *Drunken Thady*:

Before the famed year ninety eight,
In blood stamped Ireland's wayward fate;
When laws of death and transportation
Were served, like banquets, thro' the nation.
But let it pass, the tale I dwell on
Has nought to do with red rebellion;
Altho' it was a glorious ruction,
And nearly wrought our foes' destruction.
There lived and died in Limerick City,
A dame of fame, Oh! What a pity
The dames of fame should live and die,
And never learn for what, or why!
Some say her name was Brady,
And others say she was a Grady;
The devil choke their contradictions!
For truth is murdered by their fictions.
'Tis true she lived, 'tis true she died,

Home Wasn't Built in a Day

'Tis true she was a Bishop's bride,
But for herself, 'tis little matter
To whom she had been wife or daughter.
Whether of Bradys or O'Gradys!
She lived, like most ungodly ladies;
Spending his reverend lordship's treasure
Chasing the world's evil pleasure;
In love with suppers, cards and balls,
And luxurious sin of festive halls . . .

SEVENTEEN

In the late 1960s, and early 70s, life was fun, with fond memories of many happy days and nights. We loved the seasons as each of the four brought its own individual joy and entertainment. In particular, though, we loved the autumn. This was the time that the stacks of hay were brought down from the meadows to the barns. After the hay was cut, it was put into large stacks and left there to dry over the summer.

Traditionally, all the hay was brought to the barns before the Listowel races in mid-September. Many farmers went to the races after the hay was harvested. Dinny Mac Auliffe would draw the wains for Fitzgibbons' from a field in Ballycullen, a mile outside the town, to their barn beside the old Garda barracks. Transportation was by means of a horse and a type of trailer, known as a float. Every youngster in the locality would wait for Dinny on his way back from the barn to get a ride through the town on the float.

'Everyone aboard then,' Dinny would say.

A big cheer would then go up, twenty odd children screaming with delight. Dinny would then burst into song

Home Wasn't Built in a Day

Oh! Oh! oh Antonio, he's gone away,
Left me alone-ee-o, all on my own-ee-o.
I want to meet him with his new sweetheart,
Then up will go Antonio and his ice-cream cart.

Mushroom picking was another exciting autumn activity. After the hot and balmy summers, which they always seemed to be back then, the mushrooms always seemed to jump out of the ground in an instant, especially if you had a few showers of rain. Between the dampness and the heat, they would cover the fields, making them look white at times. The one thing about picking mushrooms though, was that it was a very secretive occupation. There were only certain types of fields that would produce mushrooms and only the chosen few would know where they were. When word would get out that mushrooms were out, it meant an early start, probably about six in the morning to make sure that you got the lovely buttons or 'cuppies' as we called them. I would be as proud as punch coming home with a gallon full of cuppies.

My mother would boil them in milk. She always said that there was more goodness in cooking them that way and who was I to argue with her culinary prowess. The big, flat mushrooms were delicious too, as these were full of flavour and were lovely roasted on top of the range with a bit of salt.

Melda Hanley had a sweet shop on the Quay. Her shop was a haunt for beginner smokers, as Melda sold single cigarettes. It was also a haunt for late-night revellers, as she also sold soup and bovril. It wasn't a place to visit too late, as the occasional row could break out because of the

Paddy Cronin

demon drink. God, poor old Melda stayed up to serve in the shop 'til very, very late. To make sure that she didn't sleep out the following day, she had a piece of string tied to her hand, which draped down the three storeys from her bedroom to the front door. The early callers to the shop would pull the cork to waken Melda. It used to be great fun for us pranksters though, pulling the string and getting Melda up.

Her sister, Eileen, was blind as a bat, but in spite of this, was still the librarian, next door in the library. We were not members of the library, so we used to crawl in under the counter, so Eileen couldn't see us. She wore very thick glasses, with lenses like the ends of two lemonade bottles. They didn't work too well either, as she seldom saw us sneaking in. It was so funny though, having a near-blind librarian in charge of a library.

William Joyce was an Englishman, who stayed as a lodger at Melda's every summer for four or five weeks. He had toured the south of Ireland many years before and discovered and liked the village, so had been coming ever since. One night he sat down with Melda and Eileen and confessed to a terrible crime.

'One night, while roaming the dark moors of Yorkshire, I murdered a man.'

'Oh my God' said the two old spinsters. 'Tell us more William.'

'It was a very violent death that I inflicted on a young man that crossed my path.'

'Jesus, Mary and Joseph' said Eileen as she made the sign of the Cross.' God be between us and all harm, and may his soul and all the souls of the faithful departed,

Home Wasn't Built in a Day

through the mercy of God, rest in peace, Amen. Go on, tell us more' said the two ladies.

'I fled the scene, I ran and ran and ran, but was eventually arrested by the police; I was then charged with murder and brought to the courts. The judge sentenced me to death, death by hanging, then they brought me to the gallows and put the rope around my neck.'

'And what happened next?' said Melda.

'Well' said Joyce, 'I woke up.'

Before the story ended the Hanley sisters had their minds made up that William Joyce would be evicted from their house, never to return again. They were sure that they had a murderer on their hands. The realisation that his story was only a dream brought relief all round.

In the summertime, we would get up to all sorts of mischief, but our idea of play was not always considered fun by the grown ups. We annoyed the hell out of many of our neighbours. Door-knocking was a favourite pastime. Our gang of four, Charlie, Seanie, Declan and myself would meet up and decide to target a few doors.

'We'll do Mick Murphy's tonight' said Seanie.

'Take the thread up and tie it to the knocker,' I said to Declan.

Up went Declan, tied the thread to the knocker, and jumped over the wall where we were all hiding. Then Seanie pulled the thread a couple of times. Mick Murphy opened the door and there was nobody there. Back inside he went, only for Seanie to pull the thread again.

'Enough,' I said, 'there are two old people in there.'

So Declan crept up to the door to remove the thread, but before he untied it, the devil got the better of me and

Paddy Cronin

I gave it a sharp tug. Mick Murphy opened the door and caught Declan by the scruff of the neck.

'So, you are the smart Alec, knocking at our door all evening.'

'Sorry Mr Murphy, but I was only removing the thread that Paddy Cronin put on.'

'Where is he?' said Mick Murphy.

'He has run away,' said a terrified Declan.

I was in big trouble now as Mick Murphy was our postman. Every day, when he arrived at our house with post, I scampered off, fearing that he would tell my mother of my devilment. I had already been reported to my mother for ringing a doorbell at the other side of the town. I was fascinated by doorbells. There were only a few houses in the locality that had a doorbell. I could not resist pressing those bells whenever I passed by. I would then run off like a champion sprinter.

Rural Ireland was still suffering from the fallout of emigration and unemployment of the fifties and sixties. Things were beginning to improve though, with a sort of mini-industrial revolution emerging within the country. More and more people were able to afford a television, although most people rented them. We still did not have a television in the early seventies. In April 1970, Dana won the Eurovision for Ireland with *All Kinds of Everything*.

The following morning a cousin of ours, Jimmy Cronin, who had rented a television a few weeks before the contest, declared to everyone he met, that he had seen the big event and that *Bits of Everything* won for Ireland. We all thought that his naming of the song was very funny. But sure, Jimmy was just an old man who got

Home Wasn't Built in a Day

carried away with the excitement of it all, the TV, the song contest and Ireland winning.

That same Jimmy was a very worried man a few years previously. He had worked in the local lime factory all his life and it was well-reputed that he had a very healthy life savings. In 1967, a Credit Union office opened in the upstairs of the local library. This was a huge venture and a new departure for the entire community. The rigmarole of negotiating with a bank for a loan was now a thing of the past. The Credit Union movement was sympathetic to everyone's circumstances, resulting in many people being able to borrow money for cars, holidays, house extensions and many other social needs. Jimmy decided to transfer all his life savings from the local bank to the Credit Union.

Then, one day, he was in the local Betting Office and village prankster, Donie Nestor remarked to Jimmy, 'Did I hear Jimmy that you transferred all your money into the Credit Union?'

'Oh by God I did,' said Jimmy.

Donie, being the ultimate joker, then said,

'Foolish man, Jimmy.'

'Why?' said Jimmy.

'Well,' said Donie, 'I was in the toilet of Foley's bar last night and Tom Ryan told me that he had just got a loan from the Credit Union and now he was firing it against the wall. That's your money Jimmy'

Jimmy stormed out the door of the Betting Office and made his way to Ryan's house. He immediately confronted Tom in a furious tone of voice saying, 'You'll piss none of my money against the wall!'

Poor old Jimmy thought that the hard-earned money which he invested was being handed out indiscriminately to almost anyone that wanted it. Feeling aggrieved at what might be happening to his investment, Jimmy's next port of call was to the Credit Union itself, where he was assured by the then manager, Paddy Gallagher, that his money was in safe hands, earning interest and that it was absolutely secure for his retirement.

Christmas was a very happy time, especially in the early seventies. Christmas Eve had become a very big night in our house. My mother was a wonderful cook and a master baker. Traditionally, I would invite my friends to the house after midnight Mass and she would have the ham cooked and would serve it up with her traditional soda bread. We were all well past the age for Santa at this point, so there were very few presents for Christmas, except perhaps the odd item of clothing. We were gradually phased out of the Santa thing. It was different in my parents' time. Santa was over for them when they received cinders in their stocking. Receiving cinders was the announcement that Santa would not be arriving anymore. What a cruel way to find out!

The Wren was as big a part of Christmas as Christmas Day itself. The Wren, pronounced 'The Wran' was an old Irish tradition of singing and dancing, and its origins can be traced as far back as pagan times. Traditionally, people went out on the Wren on Saint Stephen's Day, the first day after Christmas. People performed songs, dance and played music at house doors, and were usually invited in by the home owners. The ritual was also performed on the streets and in public houses. At the end of the

Home Wasn't Built in a Day

performance money was collected by the Wren Boys. Traditionally this money was collected to bury a dead wren, which they carried on the branch of a tree.

I was as young as eleven years of age when I first went out on the Wren. My cousin, Thomas, and I sang and played at every house in the village. I played an accordion and he played a mouth organ. The accordion was small, with about ten buttons. My mother had given it to me from our own shop during that Christmas. We played the same tune at every door, *The Rose of Aranmore*. 'Twas the only one we knew. Donations were small, but we also knew where the money was and how to charm. Hence, there were careful preparations before we knocked on the door of the village headmaster, Mr Jones.

'Take off the masks' said Thomas. 'Let him know who we are and let's pretend we have learned something at school. That will make him part with his money!'

So we rang Mr Jones' doorbell, and out came our headmaster with a broad smile on his face. Then in our best voice together we sang:

Ar mo ghabáil dom siar chun Droichead Uí Mhórdha,
Píce i m'dhóid 's mé 'dul i mitheal,
Cé 'chasfaí orm i gcumar ceoidh,
Ach pocán crón is é ar buile!

Ailliliú, puilliliú, ailliliú, tá 'n poc ar buile!
Ailliliú, puilliliú, ailliliú, tá 'n poc ar buile!

'Well done, men,' said Mr. Jones putting a half-crown into the box. That was more than we had made in our entire rounds throughout the village.

Paddy Cronin

I would usually go out on the Wren with my friends Declan, Charlie, Mike and Thomas. It was great to entertain people and get paid for the service too. What a day we would have! Dressing up in fancy dress was also a very novel part of the occasion. Some of us would dress up as straw boys, others in pyjamas. I preferred to be in total disguise. Being a bit shy, I liked being fully camouflaged with a face mask, to make sure that no-one would recognise me.

The boys would play the music and I'd collect the money. It was always advisable to have a *bodhrán* as one of the instruments. This Irish tambourine would make a lot of noise and announce your arrival at a pub or house in no uncertain terms. The *bodhrán* was made from the skin of a mountain goat and was manufactured and sold mainly in the west of the county, near the Kerry border. A goat was slaughtered many months before Saint Stephen's Day. It was then skinned and the skin was buried beneath the soil, and when it was seasoned and ripe, it was mounted onto a wooden frame. Once heated near an open fire, the skin contracted, and when stroked with a wooden stick it produced a very mellow sound, which proved a fine accompaniment to any Irish traditional instrument.

Our opening verse at each house or pub was an old dirge associated with the Wren. This old verse called for money to bury the little bird. In Ireland, we have great respect for the wren, so much so, that we refer to him as 'The King of the Birds'.

The Wren, the Wren, King of all birds,
Saint Stephen's day was caught in the furze,
So up with the kettle and down with the pan,
And give us a penny to bury the Wren.

Home Wasn't Built in a Day

We would travel to every village and pub in West Limerick, and usually leave Askeaton as our final stop for one almighty session in a local pub. Traditionally in Ireland, all public houses are closed on Christmas Day, so lots of people make up for lost time on Saint Stephen's Day.

One Saint Stephen's night, in the late 1960s, the drink took its toll. Trouble erupted in the village when about a hundred travellers, from nearby Rathkeale, decided to descend upon a dance which was being held in the local hall. The travellers, many of whom were home from England for Christmas, were ossified from drink. The hall was packed to the rafters with locals revelling in the Christmas celebrations. One hell of a massive fight broke out between the travellers, with chairs and bottles flying in all directions. Most locals fled for the door. Chris Nash, the local fishmonger decided to get out of the place as fast as his legs could carry him. As he made a run for the door, a young traveller lady who was heavily pregnant, thought he was about to knock her down, and she begged for mercy.

'Please, please sir, I'm expecting,' said the young lady.

'I'm fuckin expecting too,' said Nash.

'Expecting what, sir?' she said.

'A box of a fuckin' chair' said Nash.

That, sadly, was the beginning and also the end of the dances in our village hall on Saint Stephen's night.

EIGHTEEN

Any apple or pear tree was in grave danger if it was located within three miles of the village. One of our big pastimes was what was known as 'rawking' orchards. Apart from the obvious enjoyment of eating as many apples as you could, it was also great fun. It wasn't as much fun if you were in short pants though, as you usually ended up getting burnt alive from nettles and cut asunder from thorns and brambles.

A group of us, probably five or six, would gather and plot which orchard to rawk. Rawking an orchard was something to be proud of. Even at home it was not frowned upon. The fact that the word 'rawk' was mentioned meant that it was only a bit of fun and there was no real stealing involved. We would never say that we were going to rob an orchard. Later, I discovered that the word 'rawking' was derived from the old Irish *rácáil* which means robbing. In hindsight, we were robbers of the highest order. In fact, we could claim to have robbed the bank on many occasions. The local Bank of Ireland or National Bank as it was then known, had one of the finest orchards in the locality.

I can recall one particular time raiding an orchard in the locality with my friend Declan. It was a nice autumn

Home Wasn't Built in a Day

evening, when we decided to fill our jumpers with more than a meal of 'Charles Ross'. They were very sweet apples. I was the apple expert. I knew the name and taste of every apple, from my days of picking and selling them with my father. Declan and I gained access to the orchard through a door that was left unlocked by the owner, Dave Shanahan. After I had my jumper full to the brim with the delicious apples, I left through the same door. Declan decided to stay and fill every pocket.

'We'll never get the same opportunity again with the door unlocked,' he said.

As I was waiting outside for Declan, I saw Dave Shanahan coming and I scampered off. Dave duly locked the door, not knowing anybody was inside. Poor Declan had no way out with twenty-foot walls surrounding the orchard. Ten o'clock at night arrived and the alarm was raised by his family. I denied he had been with me earlier on, until after many floods of tears, the story of what had happened was dragged out of me. Declan was grounded at home for a month. What was even more amazing was, that at home, his family had a beautiful orchard anyway. It was just proof that it was the thrill of the rawk and not the taste of the apple that gave us the buzz.

We spent many an evening on a open green by the river kicking football – soccer, that is. Although soccer rules stated eleven-a-side, we often played with fifteen or more on each team. Our biggest problem at the time was to find a football to play with. Not many people had a football, except for those that used Kiwi polish to shine their shoes. That eliminated most of us. Having shoes that you polish was a luxury at the best of times. But there was always

Paddy Cronin

someone who had managed to find six empty Kiwi polish tins. The tins had to be sent off to the polish manufacturer, together with five shillings and by return post, a leather football would arrive. News would spread very quickly if someone had received a new football in the post.

We always ensured that we played a game of soccer in the local square on Friday evenings between five and six o'clock. I was in goals and the two pillars at the entrance to the Bank were the goal posts. The reason we played there on Friday evenings was so that we could have the top goal scorer from the English Top Flight, or First Division as it was then known, join in with us. Andy Mc Evoy had scored 29 goals for Blackburn Rovers in the 1964-1965 season, and to everyone's surprise, he quit the English side and signed for Limerick. To supplement his income from football, Andy drove a delivery truck for Bass beer. Each Friday evening, he would deliver barrels of Bass to Fitzgibbons' and Collins' pub in the square. Once the truck was pulled up and Andy was off-loading the beer, one of us would kick the ball in his direction. The great Mc Evoy would then join in. As the goalie, I would have full view of the proceedings and do the commentary as the action was happening;

'Sheahan, to Mc Daid, back to Cronin in goals. Cronin kicks it out and the ball is picked up in mid square by Mc Evoy. Mc Evoy looks up and finds Ryan. Ryan does his usual jinx and offloads to Mc Daid again. Mc Daid again finds Irish International Mc Evoy. Mc Evoy takes one glance of the goals and buries the ball, Cronin and all.'

Those whose parents could afford it, purchased tennis rackets from Cleary's of Dublin. Again, these were bought

Home Wasn't Built in a Day

and sent by post. Fifteen shillings was the amount required for a racket, but my mother could not afford one for me at the time. She always ensured though, that we had money for comics every week. Comics she saw as a source of knowledge and information. I could not wait each week for the *Dandy*, to read about the exploits of 'Desperate Dan' and 'Keyhole Kate' I also read the *Beano* and revelled in characters like 'Denis the Menace' and 'Roger the Dodger.' I especially looked forward to Christmas when the annuals came out. I always had my order in for the *Beano* and the *Dandy* annuals. These flew off the shelves like hot cakes. My sisters had their weekly fill of *The Bunty* and *The Judy*, which were the two main comics for girls at the time.

In the early 1970s, the infamous Charlie Madigan returned home to Askeaton, after a few years working in England. Yes, that was the same Charlie Madigan that caused the fuss and confusion on the annual pilgrimage to Knock Shrine. Madigan was one the great boomerangs of our village, wherever he went, he always managed to come back. It was to London mostly that he came and went. Charlie was never short of a yarn and after a sojourn away, he always had plenty to tell, especially in the pub while having a few pints. Even though Charlie was no more than five feet tall, his stature and exploits reached new heights after a few pints. It was often said that Charlie would be ill-advised to go outside on a windy day, as a breeze could sweep him away.

'I worked for Lizzie,' said Madigan.

'Who's Lizzie?' Charlie would be asked.

'Name of Jaysus,' said Charlie, 'the Queen of England. I

was employed as painter and decorator, but my position was totally abused and taken for granted.'

'Go on Charlie tell us more.'

'Fine, doing the paintin' and decoratin', but I was also baby-sittin' the two children, and bould brats they were at times. Me, inside baby-sittin' the two, and himself and herself out on the town. I painted the palace from top to bottom. The ceilings were the worst, but I had big scaffolding and I would lay on my back on the top of it, while one of the servants pushed me around. Herself would say I was like Michael Angelo. Of course, you know,' said Charlie, 'she called the eldest fella after me. The auld fella had great time for me too,' he said.

'Who's the auld fella, Charlie?'

'Philip, her husband,' said Madigan. 'He'd pretend to be off the fags, but while she was getting the children ready for bed, he'd send me out for a packet of Woodbines. I swore to him that I'd never tell her he was smoking. He was supposed to be off 'em for years.'

Charlie returned to England again, but for a very short stay. On returning home he had another story to tell in the pub.

'I went to a rally in Trafalgar Square. Herself was givin' a speech. About a quarter-of-a-million were there. Jaysus, she was as sharp as a knife,' said Charlie. 'She stopped in the middle of the speech and said, is that Charlie Madigan or is it my eyes that deceive me?'

About that time, cremation rather than burial, was becoming popular in England. This was to the horror of most Irish people; as if dying wasn't bad enough, being burnt as well was unthinkable. The motto here in

Home Wasn't Built in a Day

Ireland was 'we bury our dead, rather than burn them.' Cremation was especially frowned upon by the Catholic Church. Charlie, declaring his new-found English culture, announced to a full public house one evening, that he had made arrangements for his own cremation whenever he would pass away.

'I will be 'criminated' in London when I die,' said Charlie.

This brought a loud cheer from the house. Seated at the end of the pub, taking it all in, was John Culhane. John was a well-read man, but seldom got involved in any debate or argument. John, who could not resist commenting on Charlie's exploits, rose from his stool and declared in a loud voice, 'I have no doubt that Charlie Madigan is suffering from a multitude of disarranged ideas called illusions.'

Madigan immediately ran towards John Culhane and grabbed his hand; John was sure he was at least going to get a litany of abuse from Madigan if not a belt of a fist.

'Fair play to you John Culhane, said Charlie, 'tis great when someone with a bit of education speaks on my behalf.'

A slightly confused Charlie obviously misinterpreted John's comment, thinking he was being praised rather than slated.

The local Garda, Malachy Keaveney, was always on the beat. Every corner you'd turn, you'd see him walking or on his bike. An old lady called Mrs Hubbard lived in a place known as Gurt, near the river. We all thought she was the Old Mother Hubbard in the nursery rhyme. As children we would taunt her on the street and recite the old nursery rhyme, *Old Mother Hubbard*.

Paddy Cronin

Old Mother Hubbard
Went to the cupboard
To get her poor doggie a bone.
When she got there,
The cupboard was bare,
So poor little doggie had none.

Neighbours were concerned when she had not been seen for several weeks, but thought that she was with relations in Clare. Guard Keaveney was more than inquisitive and checked with her relations in Clare, only to be told they had not seen her in twelve months. Everybody was puzzled! She had disappeared from the face of the earth.

'Has anybody searched the house?' asked the Garda.

His question was met with complete silence. It was hard to believe that nobody had checked the house, but that was in fact the case. Garda Keaveney proceeded to break down the front door. He was immediately met by an horrendous odour and a decaying corpse. Mrs Hubbard had died in the chair at least three months earlier.

Malachy's inquiry and investigations led him to be known as Mc Garrett. This was after Steve McGarrett, from the television series, *Hawaii 50*, which was popular at the time. Garda Keaveney had become quite a hero with his detective work. That Mrs Hubbard had died in such circumstances was considered unusual in a small rural Irish village. People mostly had friends and neighbours to call, so for somebody to have their house locked up would have been quite unusual. However, with changing times, it was no longer the custom to leave your front door unlocked. People were not as trustworthy as before, and the need to protect your property was fast

Home Wasn't Built in a Day

becoming the norm. Ireland was changing, and not all of the changes were good. Modern Ireland was becoming cosmopolitan and businesslike. Women were no longer looking out over half doors. They were becoming an integral part of the industrial workplace. The slogan that 'A woman's place was in the home' was becoming a thing of the past. Prosperity and economics were beginning to change our way of life, sadly, with many of our traditions and culture being lost in the process.

February 15th 1971 was a momentous day for everybody. This was the day that our coinage was decimalised. For months prior to D-Day, as it was known, people were speculating and debating on how they would cope with the new currency. Some of the older folk could never grasp the new money. Paddy Dorman, a working man, who was very intelligent, was often prized for his opinion on various subjects. He was known as a man that always spoke sense. In Kennedy's pub, he was questioned by Liam Harte, who was having a pint.

'Will this new money make any difference at all, Paddy?' asked Liam

'Oh by God it will' said Dorman.

'In what way?' said Harte.

'Well', said Paddy Dorman, 'the next time that you go to Limerick City and nature calls, and you go into that toilet in the Dock Road it will cost you a new penny.'

'So what' said Harte, 'tis still only a penny.'

'Ah, said Dorman, 'now you will only get a hundred shits for the pound while in the past you got two-hundred-and-forty.'

'Jaysus,' Harte replied, 'that's a lot of shit your talkin!'

NINETEEN

Once a month the local dancehall would become 'The Ballroom of Romance.' Dancing to some of the country's top showbands would take place. One of the biggest nights, if not the biggest night ever witnessed in the local hall was when the Queen of Irish music, Bridie Gallagher played. Known as the girl from Donegal, she was Ireland's first female superstar. She had a major chart hit with *The Boys from the County Armagh*. For weeks prior to her appearance and many weeks afterwards, her famous song was rendered in many a pub.

As children, we gathered outside the hall hoping to get a glimpse of the superstar or better still, hear her sing. During many a dance, my friend, Declan Mc Daid, and I would climb a tree beside the hall to view the goings on inside. It was our first taste of the showband scene, something that was to have a major influence on us all.

We were not allowed to go to a proper dance until we were eighteen. We were however, permitted to go to a *ceili* once we reached sixteen, but we never availed of this. *Ceili's* were very Irish dance orientated, with *The Siege of Ennis* and *The Walls of Limerick* being stepped out on the floor. Between us, we did not have a step in our feet.

Home Wasn't Built in a Day

Ireland became engulfed in showband mania. You just had to turn on the wireless and tune in to Athlone, which was Radio Eireann, and you could bet your life that a showband would be playing. As youngsters we were all music connoisseurs. This mainly stemmed from listening to Radio Luxembourg underneath the blankets at night. Transistor radios had just been introduced into Ireland and one always had the radio under the covers on a Sunday night between eleven and twelve, listening to the English 'Top Twenty.' If it wasn't Radio Luxembourg that we listened to, then it was the legendary pirate station, Radio Caroline, which was transmitted from a ship off the southeast coast of England.

It was an era of music hysteria alright! Just to go outside our front door, you would hear Jackie Moran playing a drum set at his uncle's house, a few doors up from us. Jackie was the drummer in a showband which was formed locally called the 'Coyotes'. The Dundon family with Declan Mc Daid formed a folk group which even made it to the national television screens.

The biggest band locally though was the Donie Collins Band. Donie and his band were known throughout the length and breadth of Ireland. He was a celebrity in the community with his band having a hit in the charts called *Be my Guest*.

Limerick City itself was also engulfed by pop and showband frenzy. Tommy Drennan and Ger Cusack led the way in the showband scene and there was also the rock band, 'Reform' whom we all thought were never credited enough nationally. 'Granny's Intentions', also from Limerick, were known far and wide and were about

Paddy Cronin

to make it on the world stage when mysteriously they disbanded and went their separate ways.

It seemed as if everyone was into pop music. Thursday was a big day for all us pop maniacs. That was the day that the music magazine, *Spotlight* arrived in the shops. As well as selling the weekly comics, Mrs. Moran, in her shop on the bridge, also sold the *Spotlight*. The *Spotlight* gave every ounce of information on the Irish showband scene. It featured all the bands and their star singers and all the stories that surrounded them. We couldn't wait to see which band and song had made it to number one in the Top Ten.

'Oh Holy God, please don't say it's Big Tom again,' we'd all say. Then, I'd open the *Spotlight* and there it was, Big Tom and *Four Country Roads*.

The showband following had no boundaries as far as age went. Young and old alike followed them. The unique aspect of the whole scene was that everyone could discuss all aspects of the music with their parents. Parent, child, and even grandparent mimicked Brendan Bowyer's *Hucklebuck*, Eileen Reid brought a tear to everyone's eye with *I Gave my Wedding Dress Away*, and it was difficult to pass a public house without hearing some old man singing Dickie Rock's *Candy Store*.

The ballroom was the focal point of entertainment in the sixties and seventies. Indeed it was the place to meet your future wife or husband. We all lived for the showband scene and the weekly dances at the Olympic ballroom in Newcastlewest. In the hall, it was girls on the left and boys on the right.

'Will you dance?' a guy would ask a lady.

Home Wasn't Built in a Day

Sometimes he would go down through the line of women and get the same answer from all the ladies.

'No,' the first lady would say.

Then he would move on to the next lady.

'Will you dance?'

Again, 'no' would be the response.

'No, no, no,' was the answer from all the ladies.

It wasn't that the particular guy was inferior in any way, but that if the first lady refused to dance, it was very common for the rest of them to follow suit. It was as if they were making a point of 'if he's not good enough for you, he is certainly not good enough for me.' God help some of the misfortunates, no woman would dance with them. I often witnessed a young man standing in the same spot in the hall all night, eyeing up a girl. Come the end of the night he would leave the hall not having plucked up the courage to approach her. If a lady refused to dance with a man she could be reported to the management and cautioned, but in practice this never happened. No man ever wanted to take this course of action, as it would almost certainly ensure no other girl would dance with him again.

At 8pm on a Sunday night we would all board the bus for Newcastlewest. We were packed in like sardines. The fee was £1.50, bus and dance, £1 for the dance and 50p for the bus. Then, as we would reach the town of Newcastle, somebody would open the back door of the bus and there would be a mass exodus onto the street, thus saving those brave enough to make the jump, the princely sum of 50p. Each week, a top class showband would play at the venue – Dickie Rock, Red Hurley, Rob Strong, Big Tom and DJ Curtin to name but a few. At the door we'd be met by the manager and owner Joe Downes, who greeted everyone individually and thanked them for their support. Then, it was coats off and over the counter with them to Paddy Herbert, who charged 20p to mind them for the night.

It was unbelievable to see the mega-stars of show business in the flesh. The singing would start and the fun would begin.

There were a couple of famous chat-up lines if you succeeded in procuring a young lady's attention: 'Do you come here often?' or 'Would you like to be buried with my people?'

If the response was positive and you fancied her, you would request her to stay on for the next dance. If the lady stayed on for two more dances, the chances were, she would stay with you for the night. Any lady who committed to three dances was deemed to fancy you and then you would both go up to the bar for a Cadbury's snack and a bottle of orange. A bit later on, you would ask her if she fancied going out for a walk. It wasn't just a walk though; going out with a lady meant that she would give you one long, smutty kiss.

Trying to find a space down the road was always difficult, as every nook and cranny was taken up by couples courting. Even the buses that brought us to the dance would be full of couples. The drivers would always leave the buses open and they filled up in no time. There were bodies all over the seats with the sound of ears being nibbled and sloppy kisses reverberating down the aisle. All the buses would commence the journey home at half-one in the morning, so it was very important for a courting couple to leave the bus before that time. Many a couple got carried away with the occasion and ended up in the wrong village in the middle of the night. On the way home on the bus you felt proud if you managed to 'shift' a girl, even prouder if your mates taunted you about your exploits in the dancehall.

The last song of the night was always The National Anthem, followed by a very sincere 'Good night, God bless and a safe home'. The final question of the night would always be, 'Who's in Newcastle next week?'

When the band had finished playing, there was a mad rush to the stage where they would give out photographs of themselves and sign autographs. Young women screamed and burst into floods of tears just getting close to their idols.

During the summer months many local communities hosted festivals and as part of the festivities giant marquees were set up in a field as dancehalls. I often attended the marquee dance in Pallaskenry, and came home to an earful from my mother, as my shoes and clothes were covered in muck. I never enjoyed the marquee scene as much as the dancehalls, because apart from the facilities being extremely limited, the bands' true sound lacked clarity. Also, some fellas would do anything for that extra pint at a festival. It usually meant them crawling in under the canvas to avoid the entrance fee. They ended up being covered in mud from top to toe, ensuring that any lady would not be in the least bit interested in them.

The Catholic Church also had an influence on the dance scene. For the seven weeks of Lent each year there were no dances allowed. That meant that practically all the showbands took the boat to England and played over there during that period. With Lent ending on Easter Sunday, that night became one of the highlights of the dancing calendar. Mind you, it was not just the dances that were redundant during Lent. It was also forbidden for couples to get married during this holy period. This resulted in Shrove Tuesday, the day before Lent becoming a very popular day to take the vows and tie the knot.

In the early seventies, the metamorphosis of the dancehalls had begun. Ireland was entering a new era of industrial revolution. Foreign multinational industries were enticed in, with huge tax concessions by successive governments. As a result of this, people now had jobs and were becoming flush with money. More money meant that they were no longer satisfied with a bottle of orange in the ballroom. It had now become a lot more attractive to go to a hotel to watch and listen to your favourite showband. People who had never been inside the door of a hotel were now in one at least once a week. Everyone felt classy and more well-heeled. Gone were the days of being covered in mud at a marquee. Alcohol was readily available while listening to the band, with food being served as part of the show. This was usually a supper, which consisted of chicken and chips, ordinary but tasty food, that went down well after a few drinks. Unfortunately though, there was no dancing, just sitting there listening to the band. This form of entertainment was known as cabaret. It lasted for a very short time. Support dwindled and sadly, this became the end of the dances as we had known them, and alas, also, the end of the showband scene.

Home Wasn't Built in a Day

In 1972, after leaving school, I got my first job with Ferenka, a Dutch company that had located in Limerick. They manufactured steel cord which was used in the moulding of car tyres. I was employed in the office. My job was counting and collating the amount of steel used in the manufacture of the end product, which was the cord. It was my first time ever using a calculator.

My mother's biggest problem with my job was the wages. She thought that they were absolutely scandalous. No man should be earning that amount of money, not least an eighteen year old boy. I was earning £70 a month. She was afraid that I would go off the rails with such a huge amount of money at my disposal. Mind you that was my gross wages. Income tax and social insurance were deducted from my £70 leaving me with about £55.

Unfortunately, Ferenka, who was one of the first multinational companies to invest in Ireland, closed their doors after a relatively short time. At their height they employed about 1,500 people. Luckily enough, I left before that sad day arrived. It was a company that was plagued with problems right from the start. It was riddled with trade union disputes and strikes.

Around this time, the Northern Ireland troubles were at their worst, with bombs being planted at will in Ireland and the UK. On many a Monday morning, a warning phone call would be received at the Ferenka plant, saying that a bomb was about explode there within the hour. This meant total evacuation for at least four hours while the bomb squad searched the premises. Lots of the employees took shelter at a local pub called the Black Swan. There, many pints of beer were consumed before returning to the factory. It was widely thought that those phone calls were made by one of those people in the pub. It was their way of curing their sore head from the night before. Nothing ever came of the bomb scares; they were all false alarms.

No company could sustain that type of behaviour. Also, it found it increasingly more difficult to produce a quality finished product. More scrap than good product was produced. There seemed to be a lack of commitment, interest and belief all round. Some people said that it was doomed from the very beginning. Ferenka was built on the site of a fairy fort, a fact that was very much acknowledged by the company. The fort was well-preserved at the front entrance. It had a fairy tree on the fort and this had a few hundred lights on it which were constantly lit. Before Ferenka ever closed its door, those who predicted that it would never survive were proven right in the end. The fairies had finally got their own way.

I left Ferenka in July 1974 and got a job with Wyeth, an American multinational company in my native Askeaton. This company were world leaders in infant nutritionals and pharmaceuticals and still are to this day. This was a very progressive company and a great move for me. I spent thirty years with this wonderful organisation and spent most of that time in a middle management role. I opted for early retirement in May 2004, with Wyeth and its workforce contributing hugely to my prosperity and well being.

The social scene in Ireland continued to change with the introduction of a new type of venue, the night club. These late-night clubs were very much the go in Dublin and now they had arrived in rural Ireland. If cabaret had killed the showband scene, this was certainly the final nail in the coffin. These clubs were sexy and trendy with a disk jockey spinning disks from the Top Ten Hit Parade.

The club to be seen at in Limerick was the Garryowen Football Club. Garryowen was unique in that it was a night club, but there was also a very trendy live band playing there, rather than a disk jockey playing records. Garryowen was the headquarters of the famous rugby club. A group of four or five of us would go there every Saturday night. We would travel with Mike Moran. He was a few years older than us and had a car. Garryowen was very elitist. Each one of us was required to sign a log book at the door before entering the club. I was never sure if this served any real purpose, as a lot of the time we would sign a false name, just out of pure devilment. Johnny Loughnane, who was one of our group, would always sign in using his proper name. He could never see the reason or motive for us using a *nom de plume*. He was fearful that one day we would be found out and be barred from the club forever.

We were a bunch of culchies in from the county and very shy. None of us danced at the club. We were window shopping for women but seldom did anything about it. We stood there like statues at the end of the small hall waiting for something to happen, but it never did. We were well-trained from our showband days: ladies on the left, gents on the right. All of us were waiting patiently for the woman of our dreams to appear, but never had the courage to do anything positive about achieving it.

Mike's reward for bringing us to the club was a feed at the Treaty Café or as it was better known, Dirty Dicks.

Paddy Cronin

Dirty Dicks in Nicholas Street in Limerick was open until the early hours of the morning. We would all have a big fry up and all chip in to pay for Moran's. This was a ritual every Saturday night. If it wasn't Dirty Dicks it was the Café Capri in O' Connell Street. And now I wonder how I ended up with a bad stomach, a hiatus hernia and a constant bellyful of acid? I think that the frequency of greasy fish and chips and lots of fry-ups had finally taken its toll!

I continued to follow Garryowen, but in reality I probably should have supported Bohemians, as my first introduction to rugby was watching them win a Munster final in 1962. My cousin Pat Sheahan played on that great Boh's team and his father, my uncle Joe, brought me to Thomond Park to witness the famous win over Old Crescent.

Courting women was always a favourite pastime of mine, but I was useless at it. Useless, in comparison to lots of my peers. Nevertheless, I was always touting. A favourite place to bring a woman in the locality was the old ruined Franciscan Abbey. Lots of courting went on there. I was always a bit apprehensive about taking a woman there. After all, it was a holy place to do an unholy thing. My mother had told me about the many saints who were buried there; however, that did not stop me, as I still brought a few ladies there to court. Nothing more than a kiss ever went on though. We were all completely innocent as young men, as it had been drilled into us at home to respect a young lady at all times.

As prosperity grew, life still remained stressful, as ambitions were now becoming much greater. The new-found affluence born from the industrial development of the 1970s had unwittingly changed the face of Ireland as we knew it forever. Gone were the days when the farmer would bring his hay to the barn on a float, or when people wore their best clothes on a Sunday. New farming methods, had finally made life easier for the farmer, who could now afford to wear his 'Sunday best' any day he chose. Yes, Ireland is certainly different today, but remembering how it used to be will always be just a bit special.

Life was tough at times, but what life isn't? So far, it is just an ordinary one. The only difference is, that I have chosen to tell it.

EPILOGUE

Life is a long road and we are forever learning something new on its journey. However, we have to be careful not to misinterpret what people say. What somebody says to you may not always be what you perceive it to be or what they intend. Hence the story of my old friend the Barber, and his first meeting with the local creamery manager's father, Mick.

'What age are you Mick?' said the Barber.

'If the Lord spares me my health, I will be eighty-five next birthday,' said Mick.

'By God,' said the Barber 'you don't look a bit of it. How did you stay so fit?'

'Well,' said Mick 'I rowed a lot.'

'Between me and you,' said the Barber, 'I rode a lot as well, but all I got was two bad legs.'

The poor Barber had two bad legs and he attributed this affliction to spending too much time with loose women, while Mick, the Creamery Manager's father attributed his longevity to rowing boats, which he considered to be both an enjoyable hobby and a great form of exercise.

The two pastimes, of course, could not have been more different.

Home Wasn't Built in a Day

*Yet each man kills the thing he loves,
By each let this be heard,
Some do it with a bitter look,
Some with a flattering word,
The coward does it with a kiss,
The brave man with a sword!*

The Ballad of Reading Gaol
Oscar Wilde 1898